Mexico in My Heart
New & Selected Poems

Born in 1927 in Lewiston, Maine, Willis Barnstone is one of America's most prolific and highly-regarded translators and poets. He has spent extended periods in Mexico, Spain, France, England, Greece, Kenya, and China, both as a teacher and scholar. A Guggenheim fellow and former O'Connor Professor of Greek at Colgate University and Fulbright Professor at Beijing Foreign Studies University, Barnstone is now Distinguished Professor Emeritus of Comparative Literature and Spanish at Indiana University. He is the recipient of numerous awards, including four Pulitzer nominations, the NEA, NEH, ACLS, Auden Award of NY Council on the Arts, and six awards from Poetry Society of America, including the Emily Dickinson Award and the Fred Cody Life Achievement Award. Recent poetic works include *Life Watch* (BOA), *Poetics of Translation* (Yale University Press), *Ancient Greek Lyrics* (Indiana University Press), *Borges at Eighty* (New Directions), *Stickball on 88th Street* (Red Hen Press), *The Restored New Testament* (W. W. Norton), *The Gnostic Bible* (Shambhala), *The Other Bible* (Harper), and *The Secret Reader* (University Press of New England).

for Phyllis

a great lady

WILLIS BARNSTONE

Mexico in My Heart
New & Selected Poems

CARCANET

for my Mexican family: Marti Franco Barnstone,
Ronaldo Barnstone, Roberto Barnstone,
Pedro Jacobo "Jack" Suneson, Ricarda Suneson,
Mateo Barnstone, Gabriela Barnstone, Anatole Barnstone

First published in Great Britain in 2015 by
Carcanet Press Limited
Alliance House
Cross Street
Manchester M2 7AQ

www.carcanet.co.uk

We welcome your comments on our publications
Write to us at info@carcanet.co.uk

Copyright © Willis Barnstone 2015

The right of Willis Barnstone to be identified as the author of this work has been
asserted by him in accordance with the Copyright, Designs and Patents Act of
1988
All rights reserved

A CIP catalogue record for this book is available from the British Library

ISBN 978 1 78410 014 8

The publisher acknowledges financial assistance from Arts Council England

Typeset by XL Publishing Services, Exmouth
Printed and bound in England by SRP Ltd, Exeter

Contents

from Stickball on 88th Street

from Inventing China

from Life Watch

from The Secret Reader

from **African Bestiary**

from Antijournal *&* A Snow Salmon Reached The Andes Lake

from Moonbook and Sunbook

'Time on the World Tree' & Other New Poems

Dad and I Go to Mexico

The Dark Tailor

The dark tailor goes through a lot
in Boston. My dad's birth cost him
his wife, who bleeds to death one hot

August night. He is a widower
and keeps on sewing suits and skirts,
this immigrant born in the blur

of the Pale. I still invent his face,
his fury and his height, his nose
and speech. If only I could race

up the tenement steps to his door,
knock and say, 'I'm Billy, I'm ten,
you are my unseen ancestor.'

Of Bessie

Of Bessie dead the night that Dad
first breathes. The doctor never came.
The room was gloom. She was afraid.

She was a London Jew, I heard.
Morris and Bessie spoke in Yiddish,
that was my dad's first tongue. Their word

Chinese to me. No one around,
but once I see her photo, gazing
mildly at us, blonde, plump, a mound

of cloth flowers sewn on her blouse.
The picture brownish. In the squalor
she clutches her bloody sheets. The house

turns motherless, but how I wish
I could hang out with her a day,
watching her face, eating her fish.

My Father Selling the Boston Globe, 1905

My house of light bikes on loud wheels.
He works deep in the Boston T
where he sells papers, his big deal

to make it. At twelve he's quit home
and school. His house is not of light.
His father strapped and walloped him,

Morris, the short tailor. There's more,
of course. 1905, he's proud
to sell *The Boston Globe*, and door

to door he goes peddling a bunch
of mops. He makes two bits a day,
plenty for a saloon nickel lunch

with beer and all the cold cuts a kid
could want. The beer he skips.
I wonder where he sleeps. A weird

childhood. My father has no one.
His brother Sam hires him at sixteen,
but on pay day Sam pulls a gun

and father is out. I never get
to see my crooked uncle Sam.
Morris never sees me. I regret

I never knew the old man's fury,
his nose, speech and wishes.
Maybe he imagines me

some evening the way that I
invent the dark tailor stitching a suit
for me. Gas lamps dance in his eye.

When Blondie Conquers Dad

When Blondie conquers Dad in Maine,
Robert owns his own jewelry store.
They are a portrait on a plain

of grass, dressed up for happiness,
their eyes a triumph in the morning
of their hearts. Dad has the finesse

of his Sunday Packard, the glow
of sapphire. Mom is Plato's word
for beauty. I'd have let them know

how lucky they both are to be
New England birch trees by their river
falling on rocks through the city

of their marriage. True tyrants of love.
I am not born yet. Now they are gone.
The French are floating in above

the northern border, and bold green
Irish farmers flee from elf woods
and butchered soil to plains of beans

and Aroostook potatoes. Mom
and Dad quit their cheap paradise
to make it in New York. They've come

from rural squares to New York gales,
garbage cans and The Music Hall.
I watch battleships, humping whales

beyond our window, on the Hudson,
primping for war. All these great years,
my loving parents hide a dungeon

of angry money and stray sex.
Then Eden hurtles on a train
that jumps the crazy tracks and wrecks.

The Split

'38 was so much fun,
Radio City, Frank Sinatra
at the Paramount, Chico Marx sun

on the floodlit Roxy stage where
he tickles ivory and we cheer
until we cry. What atmosphere

on Maiden Lane, where Dad hangs out,
and me a kid riding the cage
of elevator merchants about

to trade the country! We live on
the Drive near lovely Joan of Arc
who sees me sled to the Hudson.

In the know, everyone is rich
till one horrible dawn I wake
to hear my father screaming, 'Bitch,

you goddam bitch!' He slams the door,
is gone. My brother in the Navy,
my sister wed. I feel a roar

of loneliness invade my lungs.
Mother and I are standing there,
a piano with its keys unstrung.

Being Alone

Being alone, alone, you grow
up quick. The drama is a pill.
Mother and I, a couple now,

are pals as always but we've had
to leave the Drive where there were kids
for Central Park South. Like Sinbad

we sailored down to two big rooms
in a snooty apartment hotel
near Mom's friends at the Essex. We loom

over the park and I watch the swans
rising from the small lakes. The zoo
is close. No children near these lawns

of Central Park. No more a child,
I ride downtown to Stuyvesant
where I am training as a wild

chemist. I read physics on the sub,
and after school I dance with Mom
or am her evening date, a sub

for Dad. But then after a year
he sneaks back every now and then
through the boiler room for fear

of snooping neighbors. At daybreak
we walk sheepish into the dawn,
to eager cars, and reach the lake

and part. O Dad! My love insane
and steady. How I wish we had
more time. Cold mornings, we are pain

and joy but finally alone.
For summer I can move in with him
in a cheap room at the Greystone,

upper Broadway. I wonder why
he pays top rent for Mom and me
while he and I wander the sky.

What to Do with Billy?

What to do with Billy? Their fear,
I've become too much of a Jew,
a New York Jew. I need veneer,

a change of speech, not use my hands.
Please, some reserve, shut up, don't hog
the talk. Strange, yes, I am not bland

but full of snot, a brat, and shy,
hurtfully shy talking to girls.
Oh well, Howard knows best. I'll try

to change. They send me to the Quakers
in Pennsylvania. The George School.
Now not the son of a watchmaker,

yet no one asks. My classmates are
Stevie Sondheim, Robert Segal,
and other wise guys. No one cares

to shape me for the Ivy League.
My farmer roommate is obscene,
turning condoms into blitzkrieg

bombs to hit Bucketballs, the old night
watchman who limps around the campus,
flash in hand, cane, and a howl right

out of the earth when he gets soaked.
We Quakers have the light. Assembly
before breakfast is to provoke

our silent bench to ecstasy,
to illumination. I sit tight.
The light never takes hold of me.

Some girls tremble, possessed by *lux
et veritas.* They stand and preach.
Later in the woods a guy pukes

the beer we've smuggled in to drink.
Spirit and fun. We have a cause.
If we have to face death, we think

we never will use arms. Gandhi
is God, and even during war
our cause is peace. Summer takes me

to an American Friends' peace camp,
an Aztec village in Mexico,
where I dig privies down in damp

muddy excrement. Good gentle Friends.
In Miacatlán some don't dance
or look at films. I share their ends

of breathing the still cup of sky.
One morning I hear the radio
(I am the guy who can get by

in Spanish) and shout the news, *We've dropped
the bomb, the war is over!* Chaos.
Our leader sends me for beer. We hop

down to the wild cantina. All
the white-pajama Indians are
also screaming crazy. A brawl

back in our hut. Eight of us jump
up on the breakfast table, guys,
and girls, with popping eyes, joined, lumped

like a Zapotec cactus bloom
on the highlands. We've dropped the bomb!
Peace fills our Quaker clinic room.

Dad at Last

Dad at last is back on his feet,
writing me from many hotels
with lofty names. He wants to meet

me soon in Boise, Idaho,
and in his white convertible
we'll hit the coast, maybe go

into old Mexico. When school
is over I hop on a train
shooting out West. Three days to fool

around in wartime cars. High racks
are jammed with bags and soldiers dead
asleep, on leave or heading back
to combat. I make sandwiches
by racing out at station stops
and buying corned beef, rolls and cheese.

I like the racket in the air,
the sailors snoring on their girlfriends,
the master beat and drumming blare

of wheels obedient to Indian clouds
rushing above our heads. I shake
my brain to take in remote shrouds

pasted on moon horizons, eyes
in cottage windows. When I wake,
Dad laughs me into dream surprise.

We'll hit the road at young daybreak.

Deep in Silver Mexico

Gone deep in silver Mexico,
there is a special providence
in the fall of a sparrow.

South of Tasco in an unpaved
village, our car, after great mountains
in yellow raincoats, where we save

a family climbing with huge sacks
of bright melons, and Indian deserts
where a bull on waterless cracks

of sand stands millennially
alone, Here is a silver center,
the source, a tiny scattering

of huts with artisans at work.
We enter a bleak motel room.
El patrón shuts the door. A berserk

bat in the unlighted room. We grope
to the window, rip the shutters
off their hinges and the bat slopes

out into the night sky. The fall
even of a bat into our fate
reveals our streets, and how we all

are strictly intermingled in
a silver pit in Mexico,
down in a black mineshaft. Again

our climb back up. Dad plays two parts,
to soar or plunge below the night.
I'm awake. Dice roll in my heart.

We Walk Around Tenochtitlán, Mexico City

We walk around Tenochtitlán,
to the sixteenth-century Zócalo
and *la Catedral* more mammoth than

San Marco; below its stone floor
of saints' tombs the old Aztec temple
of Montezuma, the gold emperor

whom Cortés stoned to death. The street
of Francisco de Madero stuns us
on our first night—caged stores complete

with silver art in midnight fire.
Next day El Monte de Piedad
(The National Pawn Shop), a treasure

from the poor. Dad finds a pearl ring
made from the moon. I speak for him,
his Spanish son. And then to sing

our happiness, a double date
with two foxy Sephardis, Adela
and her sister Marti. We eat

in the Zona Rosa, get drunk
on beer—my first date—do the town,
speeding from club to club, me sunk

in the back seat of our bright white
Buick Special. Their father in a madhouse,
as small kids the sisters sold ties

in the street. Now I am making out
with Marti. She enrages my blood,
her hands are everywhere. A shout

breaking at erotic dawn. Next day
we meet quickly. I have to catch
a Pullman to drag me all the way

back to Philly and school. Before
we kiss goodbye, she slips me
a hankie painted with a red guitar.

Three Months Later Dad Has a Wife

Three months later Dad has a wife
from Mexico. Marti with Dad
moves to Colorado for fresh life

and business. Later I see them,
svelte Marti, her bouncing wirehaired,
and a newborn martial arts gem

of a brother, Ronaldo, whom I push
in his carriage on the sidewalks
of Colorado Springs. I shush

him when he yelps. After all, let's
be fair, I am older. Dad begins
to manufacture silver goblets

in Denver. I meander to Maine
and college, a skinny freshman,
just sixteen, a diver with a brain

for calculus, and horrified
we few Jews live in a dorm ghetto
for the non-frats. I dive, I try

to pierce the sky on every leap.
John of the Cross leaps in the dark
to light, merging, and dying to sleep

with his lover, fused in black night.
Back in my room I worry. No word
from Dad. We'd always talk or write

and silence isn't good. Where is he?
Not in the West. I get a call.
New York. 'Come immediately.'

In New York Dad Is Weak and Low

In New York Dad is weak and low.
After the Crash, Mom said, she had
to knock him to the pavement so

he couldn't jump into a sub
roaring in. Now, we are alone—
it still is good—and take our grub

back in the room. We settle down
to chat. 'Dad, those were terrific days,
the two of us tramping downtown

selling gold watches and a strap.
You can pull things out of the fire.
Just start again. You're no sap.

I can stick with you through the summer too
or whenever.' But father says,
'I'm old.' 'Fifty is old?' 'Fifty-two',

he says. 'You better laugh at that
nonsense.' Mostly, it is details,
how once again he's moved too fast

and bills are killing him. And not
a bit of help from Mexico
he's counted on. We speak in cots

next to each other. Through the night
I break my brains to say something
to help him to get up and fight.

By morning he is tired, maybe cheered,
I think. 'I'm going back to school.'
'Call me.' 'I will.' I leave and fear.

Bowdoin, I Live in Winthrop

Bowdoin, I live in Winthrop Hall,
maybe the room, as I am told,
of Hawthorne. His flame holds the walls

in place. I vanish in the woods.
Bleak, mainly cold. The Upjohn Chapel
helps me think about all I've stood

against. Its meditative gloom
by the builder of Trinity Church
down on Wall Street, this upright tomb

of God gets me back to my father.
Everything does. Mom in exile
has returned to Maine to gather

with her relatives. Exam week.
I don't want to get mother upset,
so I shut my mouth, stay with my clique,

a Czech, a Frenchman and a Dane,
and then he calls. 'Hi Dad.' 'Billy,
how are you?' 'Finishing my pain-

in-the-ass finals. Almost through.'
'Billy, I need you in New York
now.' 'Dad, I don't have much to do.

How 'bout a few more days.' I am
almost pissed. 'Look, I'll come Friday.'
'No, come today.' 'But it's damn

midnight. No trains. Early tomorrow.
His voice is almost gone. 'Bill, try.'
'I'll try.' Then before I can know

how to reach him, I hear him say,
'Goodbye.' At dawn I call the hotel
where we were talking, but no way

to find him. I can only hope
he'll ring me back. Call! A week passes.
I am a monumental dope.

There Was a Call

There was a call, but I was out.
'Any message?' 'Just a number.'
I am elated, ready to shout,

and dial quickly to Colorado,
sure he's come back to make a stand.
The phone rings and rings. I don't know

who it is when someone gets on,
but he says he has worked for Bob.
'Where's Dad?' A formal voice on phone.

'Your father left New York and flew
to Mexico City. He saw Marti
to reconcile, but she was through

with him. He couldn't raise a cent.
Then flew to Denver and a loan
to stave off creditors. The bank

wouldn't help. This morning he climbed
up to the roof, folded his coat,
put his hat on top. By now the time

was noon. He stepped over the rail,
leapt from the eighth floor to the street.
Marti is coming. Please avail

yourself of a Boston-to-Denver flight.
By the way, I loved your father.'
'I did too. I failed. He was my light.'

I Went and Never Leave

I went and never leave. In May
it was, in May. 'The lark sings out,
the nightingale responds.' That way

a Spanish ballad told its tale.
I didn't want to see his face.
It wouldn't have been fair. I fail

in many ways, yet not in thought
of him, my planet among ghosts.
He's in a corner grave, but not

really. Dust isn't real. The real
is secret laughter. His. In Burma
and Bolivia we dream-meet, feel

us safe from skeptics' doomsday gleam.
In dream he is a tiger tree
perfecting the sky. I am dream,

I guess. Who knows how we have come
or go, or are right now? To dark
he fell. So young, but he's not dumb.

I hear him each morning. At night
we chat. I hear him at daybreak
when pilots call him on a flight

to danger. My dad could charm
a furnace or a coal mine not
to dump its workers into harm

and nothing shuts us up. He knows
I need him more and more.
Next week we'll stroll in Mexico.

I flunked. Yet feel him in his light-
gray suit, sporting a stickpin pearl
and grinning in our house of light.

from
Mexico in My Heart

Forgotten Children in Mexico City

Mexico D.F., 1943

I see them at midnight,
night half-mad with cold:
white cement of the street,
white children of nothing.

Who are these children
who sleep in the street?
All the doors were soiled,
all the walls were mute,
windows were tongueless,
the night without ears.

Indifference was pure
without future or past.
The brats of the moon
were asleep in the street.

Who are these children
who sleep in the street?

Sanctuary

The Indians of the black braids in Zacatecas
Or Campeche inhabit the non-time of the dry hills
And the fertile fields to the south.
Sometimes, they come to the cities with pots
Of burnished sun and colored fruits

And stand in their white cotton pajamas
Like snow volcanoes on a black plain.
The city is made for factories and markets
And stinking slums and poisoned limbs.
The city is a gold and steel dream of

A school and home on pink concrete.

In evening the Indians of the black braids
Leave unknowable city streets,
Walk back to their rich or denuded land.
While sunlight fills the ocher sky

With the remnants of ancient blood and gold,
The shattered tribes like rhapsodists wander
On the plains where the seasons have no years.
The Indian of the timeless land
Inhabits a sanctuary of the sun.

```
p   l   a   z   a
l               z
a               a
z               l
a   z   a   l   p
```

Best not to hurry in the plaza.
On Sunday the lampposts give no shade.
Evening. But no need to hurry home.
Listen to the lamp globes' colloquy.

Desert

In the desert are some morning trees.
    Some mountains,
    Some stray grass.
Boy, tell the girl with virgin braids
    Of the tedium
    Of savage sun.
You desert children know the stars
    Of the dumb stones,
    Of the spoon hills.
A daily sky of flame bakes the rocks,
    The bricks, and sets
    Your ancient roots
    In the astonished earth.

Ashen Land

Walk across the Yaqui desert. Ashen land.
Look up into fire. The sun
Has sucked the color from the hills.

This is a landscape without death,
It seems, for there is little life.
Vultures wheel over piles of rocks.

The mountains are far white walls
Of China under boring light.
Red sky. Moonlands. Yellow cacti bloom.

The bones of ancient cattle glimmer
Under a savage jaw of sunlight.
There is coolness in the dead wind.

Patio Birds in Tehantepec

The canaries clamor in the yellow air.
Sun in the red pores of the muddy tiles,
sun in small fires on the glaucous leaves.
Through the arcades and above the flowerpots,
the August sky is a bright dizzy plaza,
a quiet flame upon the old stone walls!

Nearby, a Zapotec farmer from earth and torrid
sky employs the rain god Dzahui to bloat his crop
of beans and squash and cucumbers big as oxen.
The reclusive canaries and the free parakeet
sing alone in their afternoon garden.
A white haze hangs above the still fountain.

In the calm luxuriance of the wild plants,
in the still mind of the dusty lime tree,
the seasons of birth and earth are unfelt.
The canaries clamor in the yellow air.
Sun in the red pores of the muddy tiles,
Only the clamoring birds measure time.

Oaxaca in a Ceramic Season

The dark seasonal downpour of this region
drums on banana leaves in the wild garden,
stings oily flesh of the avocado tree;
the air smells fresh like an earthenware sea.
Rain, wind. No horizon of sight or sound.
The circle of perception is water-bound,
until at once the sky opens to a dome—
a ceramic sea, clean of surf and foam.
Above the walls stunned by yellow sunlight,
smaller domes of tile appear: orange, white,
blue, black cupolas of fire. White sun.
Tedium. The sky and tile flames are one.

With Pancho Villa on the Road, 1943

At fifteen I am a keen skinny Pancho,
a ruffian rebel outlaw on the road,
a bookish ideologue, a puny Sancho
Panza plotting big crime with Dad. We rode
our Buick south through nights of Texas moon.
When we cross the border, we cheer and stop
for bread and pulque with the Indians. Soon
like Pancho we rape nuns, kill bankers, flop
at night in hideaways. Not quite, but look,
I pawn my life to wimple through the Gate
of Hell. On my first date I kiss my date.
Three months pass, she weds Dad. Pancho, no schnook,
curses us, armed us with bandoliers. We fight
foul Díaz, I lose an eye. We sing a lot.

Midnight Street Leading to the Grand Zócolo, 1943

Father and I were scandalously glad
in Mexico. War tore up Europe yet
here were two guys, he fifty, me a bad
fifteen, on double dates all to forget
our fires back home. Walking a midnight street
(where gold and onyx shone behind the glass)
leading to the great Zócalo, our feet
in brand new leather shoes entered the mass
of *la gran Catedral.* The Indians spoke
to us in Spanish, I interpreted
and Dad was proud. The saints were kind. They stared
from their great Asian eyes. A little poke
and Dad saved me from heaven. Wrongly dead
he takes my hand again. He fled, but cared.

Quaker Love in Miacatlán, 1945

The Shakers, who died out for lack of love
in sheets, made beds and chairs erect and plain,
and Friday nights they shook the rafters of
their hall with song and danced away the pain
of stark abstention. With a Quaker crew
I go to Mexico to dig some holes
and nail some wooden seats to shit into
so Zapotecs can squat and learn our roles
of hygiene. Then I quake with you. To see,
to hear, to touch, to kiss, to die with thee
in wildest sympathy! Turn off the light.
Bodies are all we are. After still night
comes birth, some light, the vast forgetting and
the blows of love. Sleep, sleep and hold my hand.

Companion Moon in a Mexican Graveyard Joining Us, 1945

She is a ball. I like to go on dates
with her. I'm a young squirt. Moon has no age.
In Miacatlán we are three village mates
lying by blue ceramic graves. But sage
and bright, she doesn't kick up a storm
at our ménage à trois. We hug. She tattoos
romantic light across our chests. Our form,
the two-backed beast of love, is new
to us. Round, trembling, our sweet milk and sweat
grow brilliant as we shake the world away
and come to secret knowing. In Mexico
a graveyard is a private place. We let
night's mercy govern us in moon shadow
by Nahua tombs, collapsing in one ray.

With the Quakers in a Cobbled Village, 1945

The Quakers schooled me. Silently we sat
until 'the inner light' got someone who
rose up and spilled it. I could never rat
on my blank soul; the meeting house was too
sedate, and I was shy. Yet Mexico
was ox and white pajama. In Miacatlán
at three the word reached us by radio:
'The bomb has dropped!' And every Quaker man
and woman wildly cheered. We drank some beers
to celebrate the word. Though pacifist
and gentle, we young work camp volunteers
foresaw an end to slaughter. Through blue sun
on our rough road of dung, I ran and kissed
the *patrón's* daughter for the war we'd won.

Winter Orphans in Mexico, 1947

The Spanish civil war, their parents dead,
a troop of refugees poured out of Spain
and docked in Mexico. I found a bed
in a white room on their roof, and got plain
beans, potato tortillas, my cot, all just
for friendship and English. I was a free
orphan like them. On evenings of young lust
I stayed out late, read books all night, a café
on Calle Delatrén where whores sat down,
the smells were milky. Manolete came,
to town to fight—sad-eyed maestro. I sold
my blood, bought a white jacket and went downtown
on a first date. We danced and knew no shame.
Back on my orphan cot we rode the bull.

In Our Life Watch

In our life watch we are down to five
or six Pierre Grange watches, a jeweler's box
of soft Swiss straps and a few
precious stones we are selling off to pay
the Greystone Hotel bill and meals.

Dad and I leave early each morning
on our rounds in the labyrinths
of narrow jewelry stores downtown.
How will we eat after our loot is gone? No worry.
Some way. I love this summer in New York,

best in my life. Not Camp Modin in Maine
with its daybreak lake and canoe trips
but real city watch shops with grownup men
we waylay and haggle with. On Sunday
we prowl Coney Island or the World's Fair.

Dad was twelve when he left home and school.
I'll soon be twelve and I've got
my father as my closest pal. We celebrate
each sale, each trade. One afternoon
with a twinkle he slaps down 300 bucks

for a diamond—most of what we have
to live on. Next day sells it for a thousand.
He finds the way. Things get so good
we spend our Sundays watching Gehrig
and DiMaggio knocking leather into the bleachers

or Peewee Reese catching the impossible.
We miss the Series when Dad goes West
but I grab wartime trains to meet him
on our swinging life watch through red
mountain states and Mexico adventures.

In Mexico City he marries a child bride
and I'm living with Spanish children
from the civil war in a barred-in orphanage
where I share a room on the roof.
Then, too soon, Dad and I talk all night

in our New York hotel. Lying on narrow beds,
we conjure up Rembrandt's beggar in baggy
nobleman's dress, how the Swedish Angel
wrestler hugs a foe till he drops inert.
Then the hill of debts. Am I father tonight?

In the morning I leave for Maine,
he's on a plane to Mexico where he must
pawn his soul for silver. No luck.
He flies to Colorado, plays a last card
at a Denver bank. Loses. Van Gogh's face

against the wall, he climbs high to the roof
where he folds his coat, places it
on a stone bench near the ledge, his hat on top.
He steps over the low railing, leaps,
and floats in blind sorrow out into May sun.

Dad's fallen again, but we can't wake early
and look up a small jewelry shop
to peddle our wares and hearts,
our soft Swiss straps or cold diamond,
since death at last has cleaned us out.

Room on the Roof of the Spanish Refugee Children's Orphanage, 1946

After my father's suicide, young Marti,
        my Mexican stepmother,
goes back to the iron bed with her mother
        Rebeca, a Sefardí
from Constantinople, who normally
        calls me *mancebito*,

young lord (in medieval Ladino),
        but she is afraid I'll get
her daughter as my father had.
        They rent some rooms behind
the great cathedral, a small hovel
        in the old district. I too

live this year in Mexico City,
        near Marti, in an orphanage.
If I can't make it back by ten
        (I give evening classes
all over the city to earn some pesos)
        I do an all nighter,

reading in a lowdown café, or better,
      go to Marti's and sleep
on a straw mat on the floor
      between the tiny Indian maid
and her brother Sam, an army captain.
      Often when I am broke

I sell my blood in a clinic, and on
      one Saturday twice—but not
in the same place. The Aztec nurse
      notices the fresh pricks
but she lets me through. Beautiful Marti
      is only three years older than me

and before my father made his move
      she was my first date.
I care for her and never know
      that the mere sale
of my blood is for her a stigma
      God will not forgive

but who could not forgive us for
      necking in the backseat
of Dad's Buick. In the morning
      as my train pulls out,
she gives me a silk handkerchief.
      Sewed on it a red guitar.

A Bohemian in Mexico City, 1947

In Mexico when I have nineteen years,
Marti, my father's widow, living here
behind the Catedral, poor, unbitter,
sends me to tango school—'and twenty years
no es nada', sings Gardel. With a soft look
I'm holding my first love and the slum street
where we sleep on the floor; evenings I shake
in the young arms of the professional
girls of the bright dance hall, who bend my arm
and push my legs around the room. Dark, tall
they rub me and I squeeze them. It is right
to burn the globe. Life is a bubble. Our feet
spin through the *ocho*, then glide without harm
across the polished floor, innocent and light.

Slum Café Playing Mousorgsky, 1947

The streets were winter high and cold
in the slum barrios where I walked
la capital to find an old
café where I could read. I talked
to no one but I heard my book
which was a mirror of an age
glaring all night. At dawn I took
the bus back to the orphanage.
Nothing happened but solitude
and lovers at the tables smoking
and waiters leaving me alone.
The rain, the youth, the cold I brood
on now again at midnight, poking
back to glass-bright tables not gone.

French Cake at Apartment of la Française, 1947

The year I sleep up on the roof in a
room I climb to by outdoor ladder, sun
wakes the snow volcanoes Popo and his La-
dy Ixtaccihuatl, who gleam at dawn.
Our orphanage has bean soup but I starve
for sweets, and when Paco takes me to eat
at a French dame's elegant digs I cave
in love for Françoise, her fat crêpes, her feet
in braces up to her knees. Smiling she urges
platters of cream cakes all afternoon on us
and plays Offenbach's *La Gaité Parisienne.*
I fall for older women. Young blood surges
between my virgin legs. Home on the bus,
squashed, cold, I ache for her sweet oxygen.

What It's Like to Burn at Nineteen, Read Dos Passos and Hemingway, and Dream of Women

At the Benjamin Franklin Library
I find hot books to keep me reading till
the dawn. Once through an art-class door I see
a naked woman posing. I freeze still
on the staircase. Women are mystical
earth beings, the alien sun in soul or in
the air where I can spoof with them. Yet all
my dreams are ignorance. I've never been
in bed with mystery. An older friend
(I'm young for her) tells me to save my juice,
she knows a *chica* on her floor who'd sleep
with me. No. But soon in blue Veracruz
the sheets of a rented room burn. We blend
our virgin thighs. Fishing is fun and deep.

Pancho, Zapata and the Trap

Pancho, with your silver pistola hot,
tú das consejo, riding down from the North.
Zapata comes up from the South. You got
The tyrant out, blood pouring from the mouth
Of México for ten years straight. Genius
At tactics, peasant hero, all the songs
Ennoble you. Zapata on white horse,
The mestizo messiah must die young.
It's better to die on your feet than live
on your knees. Earlier a colorful *charro*,
A freedom Lincoln, your trap is to fall
For Carranza's sidekick Jesús Guajardo
Whom you meet in Chinameca. A ball
Of dirty lead commends you to the stars.

The Ocean Feels Too Much Sorrow

The ocean feels too much sorrow to say hello
to me drinking hot chocolate in Veracruz,
only a few meters from her winter hats of foam
babbling by my sandals in waves of tears.

She wears a jacket of figs and drifting garbage
and a hundred years of roses whose smell covers
alleys and newspaper stands in the tropical city.
There are many rich upstairs widows mourning

officials from San Juan de Alúa and far Puebla
and hut widows mourning Indians in white pajamas,
passing their lives as companions to ox and hoe
and old widows waiting eagerly for the ocean to move

out of her pocket down their street to enter them
and drown them in dignity next to a riotous cantina.
Here, down from the Autónima, I've come a while
to know a woman in this tin roof tropical city

by the ocean who fusses. Now with my hot chocolate
favored by huapango dancers and Maya gods
and workers on the oil docks shipping black gold,
on this hot night of ocean groaning in the engravings

of Spanish slave ships slipping over throbbing hair,
the ocean and I talk heart to heart about what
to wear on Sunday morning and of street orphans
who sleep in mounds on the bad avenues

by opticians and sad venereal disease clinics.
Though hard to catch her plashing words,
the ocean voice amid her continents slows down
to a soft roar in a cup of chocolate on my table.

Night of an Exquisite Morning

I had a narrow room on the roof
of our poor pension in Mexico City.
Write me if you're alive. I'm ashamed.

You came to solitude. Your name is fragile.
I knew you vaguely at the school
and you at table where we eat together.

In the evenings I read in my white cell.
At nineteen my thighs shoot out heat
suggested this house. I'm there

like the light bulb alone above my bed.
At dawn I see Popo who is smoking slowly
like the owner of the kiosk at the corner,

seller of oranges that hide in their center
a moon green with hot plains of Veracruz.
I hear a plash of water drizzling just

outside the window. The Indian maid
is taking a shower. Her nakedness makes
prince Popo blush. She is my age. Quickly

she leaves. I'm stretched out
on my back, eyes tranquil, and the door
opens. Someone else has climbed up

the ladder to the roof. It's you. You let
your skirt drop, lift the sheet and lie on me.
You eat my mouth and sit down on

the tree that doesn't know the rain
in the center of the orange. In sun
we join, we sleep. Then you get up and leave

the air. If you're alive, I'm here on the sheet.

Sor Juana Inés de la Cruz Who After Criticism Gives Away Her Vast Library and Tends Her Sister Nuns During a Plague Until She Too Is Its Victim

When I am dead they'll say I was a muse
and praise my science and the poems condemned
by fulminating bishops who abuse
me as a bastard child, mestiza blend
of Indian criolla. Monks scrubbed the floor
two weeks to cleanse the profanation of
the prelate's house, for I (whether a whore
or nun), a female, tread his realm of love
for God. The same men beg our bodies, rage
if we refuse, and fume if we give in;
my secret love only in verse is heard.
They flattered me, painting me young, but age
is not deceived. Shade, dust, cadaver win.
Gone are the books, my loves and my stained word.

Turkey to Mexico, Colorado & the Cyclades

My dad and I each wed a woman born
in Istanbul when it was Constantinople.
Dad took an underage Spanish Jew reborn
through her own sister's passport that she stole.
I wed the Hellespont, became a Greek
and argued with the queen. They booted me
out of the school (I earned it). My chilled bleak
heart warmed in the Cyclades. Cyclops played
bouzouki for the dancing palikari.
Dad had bought Mexican silver to trade
for Colorado mountains. Long ago
he split from soul chat and old Mexico.
After half a century I still crawl
through our dream trips, his hope, his doom and fall.

Events in Chiapas, 1994

The jungle is rich in toucan,
a strident cicada orchestra,

a huge xylophone call
like Veracruz huapango.

Indians in white pajamas pray
and push the ox pulling the plow.

The hungry poor hear nothing.
A mound conceals a jade

jaguar and a cave tunnel to gold.
Men carry rifles. Chiapas jungles

are noisy with birds and bloody war.
The hungry poor sleep on mud floors.

Black Nights of Being Lost and Found

Colorado Springs, 1946

On a black night of pearl
and jackals and red earthquakes chat-
ting trembling like a girl
about to crack, my flat
was still in darkness. I lay flat

in bed, my head a pot
from Fez and Haifa. There my mom
and dad had genes from hot
Sinai and the Maghreb. Alms
to the cosmos. There my calm

was memory, but soon
I sneaked by the boiler room downstairs,
and at the street the moon
was all I saw. Somewhere
you spoke to me. My heart was noon.

No cars. The only light
the corner lamp post. There you took
my hand and we were tight
as ever in the book
of love. Toledo, now New York

not mystic Juan but you
I harbored by Hudson harbor where
I grew with you. We two
gypsies selling our wares
so we could eat and fare and spare

our earnings for a room
off Broadway where we never lost
our castle light. No gloom
of WW2 could frost
that holiday until you crossed

the country in your car.
But I trained out to Mexico.
I the child, you the star.
At night the silver glow
of storefronts bloomed the Zócalo

until we split, but not
our hearts. Father and son
had work. We were one knot.
Your gold turned lead. Light gone
you leapt to tar and raised our sun,

since we had nights and days
of unique sun lingering for years
on Indian villages. The daze
of the new renewed us and our tears
of happiness piercing the haze.

My Brother Roberto Joins Our Gang

Roberto is the last grand member of
  our family, a tickling ray
of future fun, an accident of love
  born seven months after the day
Dad jumps to death in Colorado.
  Sperm is in Marti's belly when
Dad's Sterling Silver scheme from Mexico
  breaks down. A new brother, again

a glory, now with a bilingual grace,
  he joins our mob and he remakes
the Austin skyscape, glass buildings that face
  all walls to sun. We swim in lakes
and ponds, dance Greek. He is a dreamer with
  a nifty hand in law, commerce,
a liberal Wall Street Journal voice. The myth
  is tall. Roberto's in a hearse

before we look up. He hangs in the bath.
  Our absurd planet's lost its way,
though even now on a Vancouver path
  in Canada's bright woods we say
how lucky we keep enjoying childhood pranks,
  racing junk cars, Nuevo Laredo
speed on the track, smoke in our eyes. Time spanks
  us back to nights in Mexico.

Great, Wild, Poor Jack

for my brother, Pablo Jacobo 'Jack' Suneson (1949–2015)

You are not yet born in the capital of Mexico
In the Sephardic apartment by the Cathedral
And Aztec Zócalo. I live in an orphanage but
Often sleep on the floor between uncle Captain Sam
Who snores with his sunglasses on and the tiny
Indian servant. Your mom buys a white suit
And roams from city to city; finally to Laredo
Where you see light and Puerto Vallarta where
Richard Burton burns out with Elizabeth
In their Night of the Iguana. You never get

The story of your dad, his name or country,
And so you wander Canada, Turkey, a kibbutz,
Following each false clue. My young brother is
A caballero on a blue horse, a ruddy master
Charles Dickens makes up when he tours
The New World. No one like tall Jack. A smile
Captures doves, dazzles them off roofs, a wink
Becomes a conspiracy of warmth. Good wife,
Five kids, and you partner with your sharp mom
To bring rural Mexican arts up to Gringo eyes.

I see you last at a university party for your mom.
Jubilant, you shake deep hands with everyone
From Babe Ruth to the Pope, entrancing them
With easy grace. In the crowd of noise our last
Touch is a huge embrace, and then, dumbbell
Jack, you don't take your pressure pills or who
Knows why nature is mindless and meticulously
Indifferent to life. You have a stroke burning you down,
But soon, on your stallion you hope to roar back
From mumbling hell. Your speech is plans,

Horizons, and not yet in sound mind you try
To crawl out of bed. To dress and leave? You fall
And break your crown. 'Jack and Jill go up
A fatal hill.' Twelve feet away the nurse wired
To your bed cannot hear your move until the thump.
The floor floods with your blood from Mexico.
The surgeons stick their tools in you to save
But nature strikes once more. A demon stroke
You bear and never wake again. I'm on the plane
To weep for you, great Jack, wild Jack, poor Jack.

from
From This White Island

An Island

By white walls and scent of orange leaves,
  Come, I'll tell you. I know nothing.
    By this this sea of salt and dolphins
I see but fish in a dome of sun.

In stars that nail me to a door,
  There are women with burning hair,
    And on the quay at night I feel
But hurricanes and rigid dawn.

On cobblestones at day I watch
  Some crazy seabirds fall and drown,
    And as the bodies sink to sand
I know I pay my birth with death.

I only see some plains of grass
  And sky-sleep in the crossing storks.
    I know nothing and see but fire
In the volcano of a cat's eye.

The Small White Byzantine Chapel

On this island nude and nearly treeless
(But for the few acacia trees in bloom
In the small white plazas of stone and sun
With their zones of salt and seaweed aroma),

On the far side, across the island rock
(And the dry wind and fresh donkey dung),
The cupola of the white chapel stares:
A stucco eyeball brightening the sky.

Inside are sparks and fumes of incense,
And candle flames before the iconostasis,
Where a slant-eyed Virgin leans in grief:
O points of mystery in the finite space!

Through the black air (within the whitewashed dome),
The priest leads the orphans in prayer and song.
O lifelong darkness of the finite vault,
And the white dome vainly searching the sky.

On This Greek Island

Here where the asphodels should be,
Where the beauty of the white rose
And the green-island lemon groves
Are a fragrant scar by the sea,

Here where vision came to me,
I saw the fires of lust grow,
And felt my bones lock with cold,
And heard a diving seagull scream.

Here where the asphodels should be,
I saw the crater of my soul,
And felt a lecherous repose
Of crocodile serenity;

And on this island in the sea
I saw my death and felt the blow
Of blood made cold like stone with no
Fresh asphodel to make it free.

Here where the infinite should be
I saw the crater of my soul,
And felt a lecherous repose
Of heat take hold and strangle me.

Two Landscapes

Almuñécar, Andalusia, Spain, 1951

In the stark desert of a guitar,
In sunflowers by the fertile sea,
In the nude black flesh of an olive,
I have found a monastery.

I roam the patio garden,
I hear a hill river in the large bell.
Under a pure blue cape of sky
I am not walled in by sheer walls.

Behind my eyes is desolation,
Yet near me grows a cypress
Like a brown flower on fire
Behind my eyes are black spaces.

I roam the patio garden
(There is sun on the peaceful trees)
And step within my barren mind,
Down—in flight to a sunbreak sea.

Poros Cemetery

From home of Mina Diamondopoulou, Poros, 1950

Alone, above the bay of verdant water,
Cemetery on the Cycladic island hillside;
Always distant like the tumbling gulls near town
And the citric aroma from the mainland.

By the stucco walls—eight dark cypress trees
By lean walls soaked and stained in white chalk.
The cypresses point up through the dry sphere,
Black shapes through the limpid haze of dust.

The gravestones write words on the square of land.
(They speak only to those who know their death.)
Pins of citric fragrance pierce the air
And no quiet caïque mutilates the peace.

Now

Mykonos, 1950

Be still. Be still. Open your eyes
Like still sails in a constant wind
And let the black glass of thought cloud
The daylit picture in your eyes.
Let the center dull the icon;
Shield and still the bright illusion now.

And see, now, with your pupils wide
Like the planet's unbound air, see
With a deep and desolate faith
Your fearful death and hole in dust,
Your strength and sudden ocean flights
Behind the simple lens of sight—

Be still. Be still. Open your eyes
While skies lacquer into rimless night.

I, George Seferis, This Friday of Barbary Figs, Say Hello to Blood

Spetsai, 1962

Two horses and a slow carriage outside
My window on the road to Spetsai where
I walk when everyone has gone to sleep. The air
Is salt, a gentle wind of brine and smells
From the old summer when a woman said,
'I'm no sibyl, but your asphodels,
Antigone and blossoming seas are dead.
So let's make love.' I am a diplomat
And poet, taste the archeologies
Of old statues weighing me down, yet think
Before I'm under house arrest I'll chat
And sleep with her. Help me, cut me. The sea's
live blood is better than a glass of milk.

Light and Darkness

Once past Acheron, the river of darkness,
We shall lie as bones and dust.

'Prudence', Asklepidades

I wake. Seabirds wheel overhead.
The day shines like a violet grape
In the rose sky of my eyelids.
I was sleeping on a rock beach—
Now I wake with terror and light.
Am I here? I will not be here.

One day I will sink into dark,
Down in the very bottom sea
Where now I watch islands of light
And sun shuddering in tall grass.
Just before I open my eyes
I see a vast meadow of rays.

Far in the bay as yellow sail
Looms and blurs in confusing glare,
I think of the ancient poets
Who cursed the tomb and praised sweet sun.
Halfway through life, momently blind,
I think, is this all? Who am I?

Monastery

Paris, 1949

When I wrap myself in sweet-smelling seaweed
And wade to the river below
Where my friend the supple fish
Swims alone and with open eyes,
When my gazing runs to the sea
With sun that falls in silent strands
In the still rooms of a bird's ear,

Then, a shrill crane stands up pointing in my head,
And I feel the compact rhythm, the straining sap,
The dark drum within the cypress trees,
And I walk a bit on cloudy sand
Or loll awhile in a white tortoise shell,
Holding soft mirrors of the sun
On the yellow flower in my hand,

Or wait till the tide lifts the shell
And flood sweeps me out, out,
Near the solitary gazing tern,
Near the glory of the plashing seal,
While a sky of sleeping storks
Glides softly to an endless fleet
Of giant herons rising from the surf.

Rise Outer Sun

Rise outer sun; lift the green river
Limpid to the visual ceiling.
Spread its transparent form on the woman
Of the sky, and pure lines will sing
Around warm spaces of perfection.

For within the body we are traveling
Away from the ring of flesh; inward
To the point, in-prick of blackness,
To the lost center where the great
Unseen bell chimes—silent calling.

Yet going inward, is there no return?
Near the white ball of center,
Factory-hand of dreams, immense eye,
Near the chamber of ecstasy! O
Hard voyage for the still weak.

Come, fear must die for peace.
Atop the hill, the white house—
The chamber of ecstasy.
Let us climb, let us climb
To the lighthouse of being.

After the Greek Civil War, 1949

for Vicente Aleixandre

In a dark pool hall
> ghosts sip sweet coffee.

An amputee smokes,
> whistles as he eyeballs

And shoots for the pocket.
> He wins an ouzo

And hops outside
> to the King's Park of Zappeion

Where sun falls in the still
> rooms of a bird's ear,

But no one walks
> no marble ghost on the hill.

The abandoned Parthenon
> is sleepy.

I meander a bit
> on cloudy sand

Out to the olive trees
> who wrestle an ax.

Herons rise in a terror
> from the big guns.

Cemeteries cannot
> care about the dead

Or feel the dark drum
> in the cypresses.

The dead walk about
                but fail to show.

The amputee walks about
                twirling worry beads

And wears a carnation
                in his kouros lips

All morning in memory
                of hostages in trucks.

First Christmas After the Civil War

In their Sunday-best rags
three musicians from Epiros
are waiting by our Athens door
on our big marble landing.
We let them in to play.

A cloudy Sunday of faint war,
Athens white with rare snow
conceals December's bullet holes.
Three cold musicians play
through the Christmas night.

Each wears a moon-gray shirt
over a cracked poor-man's torso.
The singer lacks two fingers;
the clarino player is blind;
the violinist has one good leg.

Grave peasants sing Byzantine carols
rolling hoarse through frost air.
We eat cucumbers and moon cheese
and dance on Thracian rugs.
When they do an island song

their passion almost leaps.
Trailing them, we traipse out
into the street, dance on snow,
ouzo in hand and dish out
drachmas, which they pocket

unsmiling. Their savior is not
born for them this evening.
Each wears a moon-gray shirt
over a cracked poor-man's torso.
Their eyes are low as they walk off.

Little Girl of Milk

Aliki in her Crib (Eight Weeks, 1956)

Little girl of milk,
    In your sleep your soar
Across the planet with the eye
Of the spotted sandpiper bird,
    Exploring island streams
    In the universe.

    The North Star is just
Beyond your fingertips,
And you reach to seize the tiny light
    And place it with the dolls and clown
    On the white carpet
    Of the world below.

When you wake to day
And the blanket house,
The white paper of your waking mind
Is marked with large fumbling objects,
And you stretch your feeling arms.

In the dark, dark era
Before your screaming birth,
Your kicks were not these giant steps
Across the easy beams of stars,
And their daywhite light,
Little girl of milk.

My Greek Girl

My Greek girl lives over there
Where the long sea glides to the serpent shore,
Where the hot sun black the sculptured rocks,
There my girl lives by a drop of water.

She resides in the history
Of that flute that shapes her olive eyes.
Her mosaic waste rests on Ravenna walls—
High narrow palm tree by ferns and bells.

My Greek girl lives over there
Where a warring angel can do no harm,
Where the heat or mountainous wind
Only makes her change her song.

She is shallow as a bird's wild cry
And deep as the paths of heaven on a seed.
Dance with your young ancient feet,
Greek woman living in a drop of water.

A Blind Beggar-Musician of Anatolia

Mr. Babi's indrawn eyelids do not move.
The watery craters scar his baby face.
They are sewn-up holes of Bible light.
Glory burns inside, yet the Devil's close.
The Devil's friends who make him trip and fall
Will grovel in the burning grease of Hell.

Dogs and cats are daughters, sons of Christ.
All love him. He loves every simple being.
He would fondle lambs, bears, tigers, lions,
Any furry, felted hide or flying thing.
Mr. Babi's fingers—firebirds in black space—
Love to rest on necks of donkeys eating grass.

Mr. Babi talks of death. He's fallen sick.
Pus and tonsillitis. He cannot swallow.
He wipes his wasted face with fevered hand.
He walks a bit and stumbles into furrows;
Wanting life and warmth and loving brothers,
He founders in a ditch of carbon flowers.

Mr. Babi's eyelids feel a blow of light
As yellow angels plummet through his sleep.
Fig trees freeze in fine silver candelabra.
The black noon flattens into fulgent seas.
The heavens open to the bright wool of summer,
And death is home, health. Death is cheap peace.

A Cheap Hotel in Plaka

Athens, July 29, 1998

A cheap hotel again. I stuff my ears
With toilet paper soaked to mute the noise
And sleep hot hours. Can't sleep. Go out for beers
In Plaka, gazing at the half moon poise
On the Propylaia. I wonder if the Parthenon
Or Annapurna is the supreme glare
On earth—marble at night or ice at dawn?
Mammoth beauty startles, hangs in the air
Of memory, and goes. I never go
Into the dark for good. Death is unknow-
able. You will know mine. Not me. Ronsard
Said, *Allons, nous.* So I get up and pack
Again, taxi mad to the boat. On board
I dream a while, watch islands from the deck.

For Death Will Come Still Too Soon, 1950

Go now to this wondrous island.
Find the pepper tree where your dream
Hammers lightning in the blue leaves
Sleep with an honest whore and know
The girl's true love, her nightly fall.
Go quickly to this wondrous isle,
And chew the apple, lick the sap
And suck the soil of this green earth.
Walk barefoot in this wondrous port,
For soon the pain and rot will come.
The sun will darken in your chest.
The sea will darken down and spread.
The sea will blacken all of space,
And you, a pin, will fall and fall.

The Taxi Waits for Me

Athens, 2004

The taxi waits for me.
I leave again for far,
the moon in my pocket,
and in my ear the sea.
The moon in my pocket
and in my ear the sea.

A sailor with no ship
goes crazy in the market.
Dying for a sweet voice,
she's nowhere on the street.
Dying for a sweet voice,
she's nowhere on the street.

The world is a napkin
and lovers are two eggs.
Time blows apart my luck,
I walk about with eyes.
Time blows apart my luck,
I walk about with eyes.

The sun is an onion
stinking of bitter dream.
Again I leave for far.
The taxi waits for me.
Again I leave for far.
The taxi waits for me.

Με περιμένει το ταξί

Αθήνα, 2004

Με περιμένει το ταξί.
Φεύγω πάλι μακριά
με το φεγγάρι στη τσέπι
και η θάλασσα στ' αυτιά.
Με το φεγγάρι στη τσέπι
καί η θάλασσα στ' αυτιά.

Ο ναύτις χωσίς κασάβι
τρελλαίνεται στήν αγορά.
Γυρεύει ωραία κοπέλλα,
δεν τη βλεπι πουθενά.
Γυρεύει ωραία κοπέλλα,
δεν τη βλεπι πουθενά.

Ο κόσμος ειναι μανδήλι,
οί εραστές δύο αβγά.
Ο χρόνος σβήνει την τύχι.
περπετώ με τα μάτια.
Ο χρόνος σβήνει την τύχι.
περπετώ με τα μάτια.

Ο ήλιος ειναι κρεμύδι,
με γλυκόπικρα ονειρα.
Πάλι φεύγω μακριά,
με περιμένει το ταξί.
Πάλι φεύγω μακριά,
με περιμένει το ταξί.

from *From This White Island* 61

Vert-le-Petit, 1950

The bright cuckoo bird reaches out
On sweet-France spring morning,
And apple trees of Vert-le-Petit
Send away white sobs of beauty
And feed us with a mystic bread.

Then male smell of ox fills our nostrils.
Our love washes through us and we quiver
In the green waves growing hot and cold,
In the turfy furrows where our bodies
Hug the ivory of the young earth.

The bright cuckoo bird reaches out!
The bright cuckoo bird calls again!

The cry rises with the wood's being
And wafts through the air to our side.
We refuse to wake, and sunlight swims
Below our eyelids as a warm-water fish,
Sinking, lulling us through dreamy union.

Chips of stars hum behind the daylight,
And black-eyed pansies in their yellow folds
Stand in tender sun that like a deer
Taps across the river glaze—and halting,
Holds the pricked air on golden spots.

Nuns' Children's Hospital in the Périgord, 1955

At high morning above the Dordogne valley—
The sunny and womanly soft meadows of castles
Of green spring and Roman stones and blue woods,
Of fresh grass, minute under vast airiness—
Morning light passes through tall glass walls
And spreads like cotton cloth in the corridors.

The hospital receives the daylight as a blessing,
Its modern rooms lit with a happier cleanness
Enveloping the children from the Périgord
Whose ravaged bodies linger in daylight sleep.
The nuns like white clouds, hover near a child,
As her breathing weakens on this full morning.

She is unknowing, as we are, why light will fail,
Why she must disappear so soon into the earth.
Sunlight reaches through glass walls to her bed;
Sunrays lie on the sheet drawn near her chin.
Her room, high on the soft and unfeeling hill,
Is filled with radiance of an almost joyful light.

Middletown Children

After the winter freeze—
The sweet sun on the sidewalk, on the walls,
On my muddy shoes, on black spongy ground
Still ungreen but finally warm—

The grass in the small town's
Graveyard begins to grow again around
The useless gate and on the shallow mounds
That sadly mark the children's plots.

A smell of earth and lilac
Wavers with the pigeons in a slow wind
That sways the violet bells of hyacinths
And spins the dust around new weeds.

The cemetery slabs
Are one hundred years above the small mounds,
So no one now remembers the young dead,
Though children still call out their voice.

from
Lives of the Poets

Catullus

Your Catullus hates and loves, and is a friend to many
    Romans. Take that stinking rogue Vicius.
His hideous mouth makes the farts of the foulest goat
    Seem like honey, or Gellius the flasher,
His tunic open all night to his mother, or Lesbia,
    Whose love I beg. For Lesbia I'm game
To journey to the trenches beyond civilization,
    To far India, to the barbaric Rhine
And even across the seas where the hairy Britons
    Live in rainy isolation. But all
Know that Catullus, with his Tivoli estate
    And Sabine refinement, is doomed
In Rome, since Lesbia (between noon and midnight) kisses
    The thighs of a hundred pin-brained
Imperial lovers. The flower of my love—for whom
    Catullus would weep if even
Her sparrow were lost—lies at the edge of the field,
    Nicked by the plow. Since we are
Viciously the same, I forgive us, and fire
    Depriving me of reason says
I want her. Yet there is someone of my own blood
    I love more, will not abandon,
And I journey to the East, to the continent
    Where Jews and Philistines contend.
Alkaios found his brother Antimenidas alive,
    His sword ivory and gold. He fought
Alongside the Babylonians, six centuries ago,
    Came home, but you my brother,
Now are mere ashes under marble. I came too late.
    I offer funeral lentils, recalling
Years we piddled away. Though you can't hear,
    Take this plate dirty with tears,
Saying, in perpetuum like the sun: 'Goodbye,
    Brother. Hello and goodbye.'

Wang Wei and the Snow

Although Wang Wei is peaceful looking at
the apricot, the moon gull and the frost
climbing the village hills, or feels the mat
of pine trees on the mountain sky, or lost
in meditation loses nature and
the outer light to sing his way through mist
inside, although Wang Wei becomes the land
and loitering rain, his mountain clouds exist
as refugees from thought and turn like mills
never exhausting time. Wang Wei also
is stuck in life, and from his hermitage
he tells a friend to walk the idle hills
alone, to swallow failure like the age-
ing year, to dream (what else is there?) of snow.

Li Bai

My comfort's in the windy moon too bright
for sleep. Finally, dead drunk, I lie down on
the naked mountain, dreaming I can write
my sorrow on the pillow of the dawn.
Although I freeze under the snow that fell
like egrets floating in the water of
this sleep, my sadness like a white gazelle
wakes by the lake. I'm ruined. I call to love
(I've heard her whisper several times) and feel
no shame for indiscretions. Since my wife
is hungry, I have sold my goods and kneel
under the mulberry tree, taking my knife
to cut my shadow from the dock. To home
I row. The sailor moon blows while I roam.

Li Qingzhao and the Moon

Reading the lonely poems of Li Qingzhao,
seeing her lying drunk, her hairpins on
the courtyard table as she mourns the bamboo
bed empty of her legal lover, gone
beyond the sky and her apricot tree,
I know those geese and bugles that explode
her evening in the late Song dynasty
signal her unique sorrow on the road
of the blue lotus. By the Eastern Wall
her lord and friend fell into mist. Yet in
that same small garden of their scholar's house
they'd shared a passion for old scrolls, and when
he went (turning her moon to ink), in all
the world her grieving happened only once.

One Morning in Málaga the Poet Gabirol

Eleventh century in southern Spain,
a Jew scrawls a green poem, talks Arabic
in the white sun. No wind. With ink of rain
and lightning quill he storms the moon. Then quick
as his dream lover's hips of fire, he drops
down from the scarlet night to sun and white
adobe walls. Gabirol paints the crops
of lime and olive trees in Hebrew light
of old Jerusalem. Yet why scrawl in
that fossil tongue? For God who paints the soul
with glyphs? Solomon Ibn Gabirol
scribbles for God and us. All poets do.
Happy, cantankerous, he shares our sin:
he writes for Sol. Then maybe God and you.

Basho

I write no last poem.
Dreaming thin rain on bleak hills,
Each line is my last.

Izumi Shikabu and Her Diary

Read my diary. I don't care
any more who knows
why I hate my pillow,
a moon smelling of you
like a memory of oranges.

I woke in my young life
on a road of darkness.
I can't walk to you.
Bells from the mountain
say I'm utterly lost.

I'm sorry you suffer too
yet how glad I am!
Like bamboo I'm everywhere
as you wear out
the night with my face.

Prince, here in this world
my bed is ready
for scandal. What else
is there? With you
I'll lie down anywhere.

Is the moon in prison
since it obeys
laws? Each night
I hear great hail dropping
wilding from the moon.

I'll go to you by
horse and no one
will guess I am crazy.
If you are not there
I won't die tonight.

In some places they kill
lovers. A sweet story
for poets. Do come.
I hunger and am safe
even if they destroy me.

Someone may gaze at stars
after you and I
are burned by the temple
Be calm and come now
so stars will remember.

Kabir the Wanderer

I can't weave in Benares. They threw me out
and many villages and towns say,
'Go away, mystic of no caste or religion.
You are like the nameless animals.'
They are right.
My sisters are Muslims and Hindus who have lost their names.
I carry a lamp. At night my lovers show me their breasts,
        their loins, their hair.
None has the word of Allah written on her.
None has a Veda chanting in her soul
yet we share the joy of the dumb beasts.

At dawn the sun is a gentle pearl
nameless as we were when we came through the great door
        of being
or when we leave by way of darkness.

Kabir says: There is no place for words at death
when planets drop through our fingers.

George Herbert and His Letter to His Lord

I wrote a letter to my Lord
But couldn't spell the holy Name:
'What can I do against the Sword
Lost in my flesh I cannot tame?'
The Lord answered (although I never
Posted my word to Him), and said:
'The Sword is nothing if whenever
You rave with Lust you let the lead
Of Heaven's glass be cut and crazed
So Light will magnify your Soul.'
I sealed the letter and was dazed
Before my Lord who filled the hole
Made by the Blade with Angel Breath
And cured me with an early death.

I Andrew Marvell Offer This Elegy to John Milton, Companion and Blind Secretary of the Commonwealth

Milton, you are not gentle, for
You use a sledgehammer to roar
Against the gelid walls of Hell
Or crack the crystal citadel
Of Heaven, but to me you are
An age's soul and her wild myrrh.

I see you fumble on the grass,
Seeking your saint. You let her pass
From your arms but when you woke,
She fled, and once again the yoke
Of solitude fixed you in night,
Though in your sorrow came a light,

Glowing from Eden, a green place
Below the shade of that live space
Behind the desert orbits of
Your eyes: a golden night of love,
With lanterns for the stubborn mind
Of Freedom, where no one is blind

There, my dear Milton, friend of shade,
Who nearly kissed the axe's blade,
With your dead eyes you held the sun
Of outraged Samson, bend and done
With noon. I moved our hand until
Came Mr. Gout; your hand grew still.

I find my heavens in some ripe
Luscious apples, and melons wipe
My mouth with wine I stumble on
A paradise, a virgin's dawn,
Under my feet. In my scant verse
Throbs my small garden's universe.

You dwell upon the handsomest
Of angels, outlawed Satan, blessed
And later cursed, your hero in
A sapphire world. Where you have been,
The golden lamp under the Sea
Helps God find His eternity.

Thomas Traherne on Earth

How Lucky was my Birth!
My Mother put me on a Blue, Green Pearl
    Which Atlases call EARTH
And left me on this Temperate Star to curl
    Into a Child
Of Bright Felicity, Roaring and Wild.

I came on Grass, a Tree,
On cottages with Luminous Walls of Glass
    Where shone ETERNITY
And yet amidst this Bliss I couldn't pass
    Above the Sun
to be at the Sweet Source where lives No One,

No One but Dame White Rose,
The BLOOM who was the Mother of my Soul,
    White corn her Bed, she chose
To be Remote, Invisible, a Goal,
    A Sabbath Drum
For us thirsting the Waters of her gleam.

And so I wept and grew
And angrily became a Man. My heart
    Was Iron; Lead my Shoe
Which sank me into MUD. I was a Cart
    Of Dross, and Free
Only to see Dead Wheels of Misery.

After a Thousand Years
In Ponderous Clothes, my Mediating EYE
    Failed to glimpse other Spheres.
My Spectacle was an Abysmal Sty
    Of Pigs, my Home
The Vomit of a Sea of Stinking Foam!

And so I turned my Gaze
To the Lost Child inside who nothing knew
But living Placid Days,
Who fed a ROSE on Mountain Pools of Dew
From Eden's Book.
Nothing he knew, and soon the Pages shook.

I read the Lettered Tree
Of life and found no Words, but Unafraid,
With Earth's Lucidity,
I fed the Loving ROSE deep in the Shade
Of the dumb Soul
And as Child I danced about my Hole.

Luis de León in a Prison Cell in Valladolid

Outside my Inquisition cell, the stars
and cypresses are gossiping. Castile
under the song of planets, of the spheres
climbing the night up to a sapphire wheel
of farther spheres. A week ago the mules,
farting, whining, carried me to the coast.
I suffer creatures better than the fools
who lied me into prison, who would roast
me for my Judaizing texts. Like John's,
whose cell is a cold sardine closet, who
inhabits dark-soul night, my night is day
even without a candle near. White dawns
of night! I drink the Song of Songs the way
a bird escapes, painting my jail sky-blue.

John of the Cross in Spring

After the dungeon and the whips, the night
of the Toledo fish room where I close
my eyes and am a woman pierced by light
that kills and gives no pain, again I doze
here in Granada on the hill, a whore
of God. Illumination comes and then
I soar, leaving for days. Only the floor
of the old Moorish convent feels me when
I vanish, happy. Peak of happiness
in the Granada spring of lions! Snow
of almond buds and mountain herbs! The sun
cavernously inside! My secret NO
is holy, white, ineffable. I've won
from death a spring frozen in secret YES.

John of the Cross Laughed on the Stairs

Saint John laughed on the stairs, a mystic child
with sun waking the wine. When cancer woke
his ulcerous skin, he chose to be reviled
in Úbeda. Nothing could paint the smoke
of his one candle dark. In his black cell
he drank the science of his obscure love,
who came, who joined him and serenely fell
with him untellably. The black above
the earth was daybreak in his blood. San Juan
sat on the floor, babbled, and lived beyond
the word. Felicitous. The abscessed flesh
was nothing. 1591. A pond
of light. He drank the body of love, its fresh
illusion. Until death he lived with dawn.

Limping Quevedo Walled in by Time

Limping Francisco de Quevedo pleads:
he is a was, a will be, and a wear-
y is. Nimble philosopher, he feeds
us all. Our past is vague, a dirty tear.
We dream a kinder future, but are trapped
in ticking nows. I wonder what I am
or was or will be. Quevedo, the prince
of colorful adventures, the great ham
of dames and metaphysics, who will rinse
his enemies in verbal shit, remains
my maestro just as San Juan de la Cruz,
mystic of the dark night, floats on a plain
of blind ecstatic love. Dying to life,
he's free of time and rises into light,
to an eternal now, merged in his love.
Till zapped these Spaniards invent time. Their strife
means dungeons where Juan and Quevedo write
their glory verse of eagle tamed by dove.

Daydreaming of Anne Bradstreet and Her Eight Birds Hatcht in One Nest

Anne Bradstreet and eight kids, your house burns down
near Ipswich, but with faith you bless the Lord
for each child he turns cold. Beasts cry concord
in the forests of New England, and each town
sings Sunday glory to white God. How far
we are this winter, Anne, domestic friend,
who can't know me or my three birds. I send
my admiration and a Christmas jar
of honey for your offspring (which you can't
accept, because of unresponsive time).
With all your books flaming in natural crime,

you sing of nakedness: an immigrant
to Heaven. I'm not reborn, but dream a plan
of forests, milk, and naked Mistress Anne.

William Blake Composes the Grand Design

In the beginning is the light,
the word, the atom, a long string
of black stars jammed into a night
until a bell explodes. Stars sing
out of their rings, big globes of flame
racing to everywhere. One is
the mother Sun, and from her came

son Earth and daughter Moon, who whiz
around each other and cool down
to make our blue planet a sphere
with tasty air and shifty gown
of clouds and fish, and then a deer
and elephant, and the big-brained
baboons who soon sing and compose

an opera. Those bosons trained
our gravity so we repose
and leap, and don't fly off to Mars
or to black space where we were born.
Our cosmos is composed of stars
designed by William Blake, forlorn
because all children on his globe

can't leap with lambs. The sweepers Dick,
Joe, Ned & Jack in coffin robe
cry weep, weep, weep, when they fall sick
and in chimneys choke. Mayors frown
but William knows his quatrains fail
till he makes mills no pauper's jail
and cuts all gallows children down.

Our White House

Charles Baudelaire, trans. WB

Outside the city I have not forgot
Our white house, small but in a peaceful lot,
The chipped Pomona and old Venus dim
In a cramped grove hiding their naked limbs.
The evening sun was dazzling and superb
Behind the pane. There its immense eye burned
And seemed—wide open in the curious sky—
To ponder our long silent meals. Lovely
Reflecting candlelight scattered and merged
On frugal tablecloth and curtain serge.

Baudelaire in His Paris Streets

Charles Baudelaire descends to the suburbs of the city,
ennobles the hazard fate of the vilest things,
presents himself as king with no trumpets,
valets or friendly criminals,
hangs out in bloody hospitals and pompous palaces.
In Paris Charles (who dies young) knows both hovel
and fine rooms, and the hungry fields
where the cruel sun beats wheat into rhyme.

The poet stumbles words against the dreaming pavements.
He flees to Brussels, with exiled Victor Hugo,
to escape his creditors who would slam him in jail.
He sells his antique clock to buy milk in the market
for his Belgium cat. He composes in rain and slop,
hearing the coal smoke talkative in roof tiles
while the mélange of prostitutes and nuns fans
through the night alleys. Head over his desk,
the poet wants to sleep like an astrologer along the sky

and hear an eternity of bells gamble for a rag-collector's heart,
when suddenly in his tenebrous streets, the cold coffined sun
rises through the exhausted dawn to glare black hope.

Walt, Foaming from the Mouth, 1892

Don't be surprised. I'm still hanging around,
talking to you. You thought me dead. I am
cheerfully in your room. I'm lost and found
and found and lost. A red faced man, a ham,
and yet I'm laughing in the mountain air
out with my night bats floating. Don't be sick.
I failed. Emerson liked me, yet his care
cooled after one brave letter. Did he stick
by me? Why should he? Loudmouth, I contain
too much, embarrassing my friends. I shout
and whisper in your soul, and what you own
will rot, but not my words. When time speaks out
and death demands, do not go blank. The stain
of grass is deep. With me you're not alone.

Cavafy on His Own Bed Above a Poor Taverna

The Jews and Christians of this city hound
me with their cults. 'Despise those marble limbs
and worship the unseen.' Bigots. They've found
an ally in Plotinos and their hymns
sing of a diamond heaven. It's no light
for my illicit afternoons whose sun
is candle weak, corrupt, and erudite
with kisses gambled on a strange bed. Son
of passion, I'm spent like burnt tobacco for

these nights of bloody thighs and lips. I use
a chaste demotic Greek and long ago
entombed my name in candid poems. I choose
the old city as my metaphor to know
rare limbs, old kings, and me, time's aging whore.

Arthur Rimbaud

When you are fifteen you wander far
on blue summer evenings, intimate
with wheat, pissing toward the brown skies
far and very high, your pockets torn,
your naked neck bathed in fresh air
of dusk, happy as if with a woman.

Later you go to Paris but miss Paul
at the station and foot it alone
to his house, put your muddy boots
on Madame Verlaine's bedspread
which once was white and now muck.
This sheet of marriage is the ruin

of Madame Verlaine. You sleep
with her weak husband, stab
the hand of a Parnassian poet
reading at a banquet. On waking
you kiss the dawn. It is noon.
You see a minaret at the bottom

of a well, cathedrals in a lake
and angels over pastures
of emerald and steel. You are
a child mystic. You are God.

Verlaine charms and revolts you
with his cowardly weaknesses,
but you write scriptures.
The unknown demands inventions:
the new. After a season
in hell—you the infernal groom

with the foolish virgin—
after your hunger to climb a tower
and weep in the green mist
and hazels and invent
vowels and wait for the time
when love seizes, then dine

on rocks, coal, iron, the air—
O happiness O seasons O
castles! After the tenderness
of impossible eternity
of the sea mixed with the sun,
you cease being God, measure

your disgust with flight
from youth visions. Goodbye
old Europe. Good morning Africa.
A physical man in the sun.

*

No one sees you again after
you disappear from Cyprus.
By boat you sail down the Red Sea,
then dwell in a fearful fever,
syphilis and inactivity.
In Zimbabwe a young woman

from the Harare tribe
lives with you for a year.
You care for her, almost happy
but you need money. The King
Menelek of Shoa fleeces you
in gun running, though maybe

you get some money out of
slave trading. You believe in science
and your companion servant
Djami. It would be good
to learn the piano, perhaps
have a son fully educated to be

an engineer. The botany
of Ethiopia deserves articles
in learned journals. Here
in Harar you live with rotten
food among corrupt natives.
No mail, no highway,

three souls on a camel.
The climate is good but the tumor
dangerous. After atrocious pain
you hire a caravan to
carry you on a stretcher
to Aden, the horrible rock.

*

'My dear sister Isabelle,
in Marseilles they cut off
my leg. I am completely
paralyzed, unhappy,
and helpless like a dog.
I would like to go home

for a while to Roche
where it's cool, but tomorrow I die.
Please send three thousand francs
to Djami. For you, my love,
I have assigned my last shipment
of uncut sapphires and tusks.'

Guillaume Apollinaire and War

Everywhere the wounded.
        Their screams are
                common like clouds.
A choir of machineguns
        plays a fatal tune
                on Gallic skulls. A Kraut
mortar gets me.
        Soaked and dreaming
                in the trench, my head
is shrapnel. They trepan
        my skull.
                I'm proud of the
bandages.
        Picasso sketches them.
                Will I stroll
again along the Seine?
        After the war
                and back in Paris,
a little paralyzed,
        I faint often
                but the same madness
blesses me. I marry
        the pretty Russian.
                Happy Apollinaire.
The Spanish flu
        finds me weak

                        in the thirty-eighth year
of life, the terrible year
            for the poets. This artillery
                    captain in his bed
quickly loses color.
            The plague is in my blood.
                    'Save me, doctor.
Spare me.
        I have so much
                    in me I want to say.'
But the Pont Neuf breaks.

Antonio

Antonio is my poet. Machado
the big sloppy Sevillano,
grave as a dying child and funny
like a bright orange. He
never yells or weeps or makes up
a thing. But he lives in
a dreaming stork, a hill or poplar
or in his far Chinese love
whom he meets only a few times
when lightning fills his room.
A mountain burns in him, and lonely
Antonio walks in blue
lands and sun, in the dream and wheat
of childhood. He is so
grave with round feeling, no one is
as quiet as deep Machado.

Antonio Machado in Soria, Jotting Lines in a Copybook

Walking in Old Castile, a widower
and young schoolmaster in my dirty clothes,
gravely I recreate my Leonor
who left me in the spring. I almost loath
the adolescent fields, merino sheep,
blue peaks, the first whitening brambles, plums,
your child voice in my ear, yet walking numbs
intolerable whispers of the bed. To keep
your face, it's best to learn to wait. I will
know victory (or so the proverbs go)
and see an elm that lightning might ignite
and char. Dry elm a century on the hill,
still graced with green leaves, I would also know
another miracle of spring and light.

Antonio Machado in Segovia, Daydreaming of Soria, Baeza, and Sevilla

My window grins over the crypt of John
of the Cross's bones down in the cypress grove.
I'm living up the hill in a small room on
the Street of Abandoned Children. I keep a stove
under the round table, a blanket on my knees,
and each night scrawl till dawn, throwing away
the papers with their dream of orange trees.
The hunched lady scrubs my ashes off the gray
floor and toilet's red clay bowl. My cell,
the dream ground of a Chaplin walking man,
has (like Saint John's cell) a cot, chair, and field
around for solitude. The Andalusian
fountains laugh blue. My eyes, a lost moonbell,
are grave and funny like an orphan child.

Rilke in His Doctor's Arms

Those blue plains, the white horse
stumbling in Russian twilight.
There Rilke goes with Lou in his course
in adult love and voyage
to be the lifelong dragoman of the road
till at Muzot he is a hermit sage
in dapper lonely clothes, writing in a cold room,
hanging on in pain alone. He takes a break,
goes to Paris for some months—his happiest—
with hope of cure through friendships.
Lastly at the Swiss clinic. When the angel of harm
comes to his shell, he boards a ship of night
and dies, his eyes open, in his doctor's arms.

Borges and His Beasts

Something is wrong with your face. No, it's not
an old man, but one who has not grown up.
Despite gray hair or one eye caved like a cup
and dead, and one eye that is a gray plot
of yellowish mist through which a white deer
leaps and fades or flashes blue in a dream
where you forgot your death, you longly scheme
the alphabet of light to fill the sphere
in your heart. Blackness gone, now you must smile
like a child. You relish an Old Norse word
offered the sky. But lonely and absurd
you know something is wrong. Face of a child,
laughing, tormented like a tooth, your eye
waters to know the panther who cannot die.

Two Borgeses

Old man from the North, immaculate liar,
your iron helmet and the deadened eyes
waken at dawn, and watch red spears take fire
and fade on Danish beaches. You despise
the lazy, learned man moving in gentle
amazement with a cane, who keeps a gold
watch in his coat so he can lose the mental
con game with time. You feel remorse for old
Jorge Luis Borges, outwitting God,
Persians, and the algebra of being. Both of
you hunt like madmen for a word. Your love
is hidden, though it burns behind the sword
of Norsemen and the cane. You are a fraud
and friend, a haunting brain and lonely lord.

Evening Talk with Borges in Buenos Aires, 1975

Evenings we set out for a restaurant,
Maxim's or the Saint James Café. Maxim's
is not where Proust and Jean Cocteau might plant
their heels and chat, yet it boasts blond Nazis
in khaki shorts, conspiring in the rear about
inferior blood. I say I want to sock
them, but Borges says, 'Be serious. Pull out
a knife.' Good writers spill romantic talk.
When a thief pulls a gun on him and warns,
La bolsa o la vida, he says, *La vida*.
The villain flees. We take a stroll. He mourns
the better days. 'That's illusion too.' Cheetah-
time bounces about. Borges is alive
and writes. Death walks with us but can't arrive.
Death walks with us. Death can't arrive.

On Antoine de Saint-Exupéry's Orphan Prince

The little prince voyages right
up to asteroids, shares a bit
with an astrologer and a drunk
seated in the sky, high on junk,
but his courageous old man flies
off for France, is shot down and dies.
A war pilot risking whimsy,
his iron dad writes below the sea.

Last Voyage of Hart Crane

The rose tarantula is hanging from
The window of my Aztec house   the worm
Sleeps in the bottle of mescal   I come
Drunk as a white volcano   my dead sperm

Finds no black stars in hell   O Lord,
I'm on the floor! the lily is my sun
Tricking me into hope   I am the ward
Of brutal bells that ice the broken dawn

With clanging nails of crucifixion yet
In this bronze noon my old Indian friend
Affirms me mildly through the alphabet
Of resurrection   carillons offend

The pit of truth   I wake   O Lord   I wake
But not to azure dawn   how many nights
Must I ride with the hurricane? The snake
I wear—the smutty serpent chills and lights

My tongue's despair   its campaniles and lutes
Shower me with glass   I see the firmament
Still green   Save me   I'm floating   Love pollutes
Eternity! Go home? Pesos I've spent

On boys. Woman, receive me in your hands.
The belly of the Sea invites my gaze.
Snow lies on its rite moon   a kitten lands
On me   it gently cries for me. I praise

The Heaven of the Jews   let us the Weak
Find Mercy in her Sighs. Tomorrow when
I say goodbye to her, maybe I'll seek
A way back up when I have cast my pen

And me into the cruelly pious hope
Of waves. Or when my visionary love
Our argosy casts me to the caving rope,
Maybe I'll let the dogfish drift above.

William Carlos Williams Back in Puerto Rico

Well Jersey is still a yellow place
May comes to with rain washing
chickens and pots of flowers
and New England—delicate rust
and immaculate white beds—
but back in old San Juan

it's beautiful as a baseball
game or Spanish Jews—I have some
of their blood too—escaping
laughing from the Inquisition.
Here slums are magnificent
baroque and golden red stone,

and what makes me happier than
the Pleiades is the skinny rubber tree
with big boobs and milk under
the skin all out in my back
yard or up in the tropical rain
forest. There pines are friends

and cool even to cranky old men
named Alfredo or Carlos
who walk with shaggy nostalgia
like the poor ascending home
where they listen to the radio,
make love, and iron new clothes.

George Seferis in Holy Athens, 1949

Kimon Friar was walking arm in arm
smiling with George Seferis. He flagged me,
'Willis, do you know the poet? Reveal your charm.'
Flushed, I said, 'I read your *King of Asine*
in Paris. *All morning long we looked around
the citadel.*' Seferis was surprised. After the coup
when Greece sank below the dictators' shadow,
Seferis, who condemned the four colonels,
was five years under house arrest. The day
of his release, we spent the evening partying
at his house. When George died, the colonels
were near collapse. His funeral procession—
a protest against tyranny—flooded the city
in the largest march in Athens since poet Solon
freed Greek slaves and invented democracy.

Wallace Stevens in First Spring in France

Brussels is cold and its stone houses brown
Because winter has let winds crumble over it,
Turning a day cloud into an illusion of crows,

But on my first day, my first life, in Europe
I chose France, la Douce France, and its green
Canopy of meditation over the hazel trees

That suits a man of seventy who has looked
Into books and around books in his Connecticut
Habitat, and at last asks to walk the fields

Of the invisible. Was I frozen all these years
Like a glittering black letter fixed by law
On a legal document? Was the innocent

Of measured paradise existing in colorful
Fact on the sandy circus of the spirit,
Yet never in the holiness of the wanderer?

Even now a scholar will say I only dreamt
Of a bridge at Avignon, of a river where cows
Waited close by for sun to feed their shade.

Will the scholar of one candle care for real
Berries that I discover amid the ferns?
No. He will say I am a creature of Hartford,

Animal of lucid melancholy with words,
Solitude and a single destiny of flame
On Monday dawn, and a beast who never went

Into the greenness of his meticulous dream.
He will say I am poor as the vulgate bricks
By my windows. He will say I am helpless

Like the shoemaker Böhme or the lens-grinding
Jew from Holland, Spinoza, whose stars were all
The World, who never left the hyacinths

Of Amsterdam. And he'll be wrong. I will claim
Sunburst in a rouge at Saint-Jean-de-Luz,
Peasant bread, a blue franc note whose fine lines

Create a woman looking Greek, anciently free
And robust. But the erudite will laugh
Since he is scrupulously informed and claim

These very tercets false and not by me. How shabby
To test my passport against the Mancha of
Don Quijote, a glassy imagination, and Sweet

France. Yet I have won, and the reader knows
In this gentle instant we are walking *chemins*
Along the Rhône, born in a solemn glacier

At Valais, and in my palpable enthusiasm
For its transparent shape I have gone too close
And soaked my shoes on its spring muddy bank.

On the horizon I watch the crystal mind
Of the firmament setting gold down with sudden
Authority of sunrays in a windowless room.

Ezra Turns Silent

'Vienna contains a mixture of races.'

– Canto XXXVIII

In London 1910 each foggy Thursday, Pound
and Waley sip rum and supper together.
From the master Sinologist, Ezra has found

China, the calligraphic character, the old. Strange
how deep the loyalty with his friend Sir Arthur,
the Viennese Jew who gives him new range.

In early cantos and the Pisan, Ezra is sublime
though already fulminating against Adams'
paper currency, kikes and other slime

and slop like 'niggers scaling an obstacle fence'.
A man on whom the sun has gone down,
from mountain forests full of light he has no defense,

when shipped home, not in the outdoor cage
in Pisa where he stalked and climbed the skyscraper
of colorful obscurity, but a traitor in a ward. Sage

mad Ezra Pound of fragments of bright trash
and sorrow in his last cantos. *I lost*
my center, fighting the world: The dreams clash

and are shattered. I tried to make a paradiso
terrestre. When he goes free, he turns mum,
and cannot turn as he steps darkly to his boat.

In Frogland i ee cummings

In Frogland i ee cummings
after a devil's island pimp weeps
& cons me in Club Venus
where one big signboard sighs
                    ON EST NU,
hire a hack i relieve myself out the back)
but a flic nails me charges me
            with crime
:vot ist meine crime, M. le flic?
Monsieur, vous avez pissé sur la France

i am young c'est paris la guerre est finie
ladies come from cambridge reds devour la russie
wops jews play with madame
            Death
and me froggy
                yank
in la belle France furiously drink onion soup
by the rivers of les Halles before
dawn's vegetable light
with ohsowearyladiesofthenight
who me wake
            to the bur-
den of being as criminal as villon ,broke as baudelaire
,springcrazy as my father geniusof joy
& *CALLIGRAMMES*
        & who's my oh! daddymaster)
GUILLAUME APOLLINAIRE

Where Federico Eats Melons the Cow Jumps Over the Moon

The sun wears sheets of bestial light
hanging fresh in the woods, but where
is Lorca's moon? Must it be night
for moons to be? By day she's there,
a ghost of memory. In Spain
she glows for Federico. No,
she is his tombstone fire of pain
and passion. A cold moon rainbow
washes his dawn. The jumpy cow
sighs for him, wants moon plants to feast on,
leaps into felicity,
munches high sky grass, but no beast
can taste his old light. Who's left now
to help the murdered poet see?

Lorca at the Well of Black Waters (1898–1936)

In gay April Federico left Holy Week for
his dark love. He wed grasshoppers on
      the orange tree sun. Soul and earth.

As a memento he put his spearmint guitar
in a weathercock spinning eternally
      over the stallion sea.

In grave July generals Mola and Franco
crossed from Spanish Morocco with bomb
      and cross. Bulls of blood.

and death. Lampposts froze in Granada.
Lorca got off a train, hid in a friend's
      attic. The Fascia gale found him.

He was handcuffed to two anarchist
bullfighters and a blind schoolteacher.
        Even Falla couldn't save him.

Lorca took extra bullets in the ass
for being *a mariposa* (butterfly). 'Give him
        more *coffee!* Code for *lead.*

At Fuente Grande before dawn, below olive trees,
not by his piano, not in his best café,
        Lorca's blood became ink,

our ink in books, and sounded in eyes
on stage. At five in the black morning,
        Federico, at exactly five,

in August '36 at five on the dot in the
heart of the ignominious morning,
        Granada's poet left the black moon

under his olive trees by the small cemetery's
execution wall. Sighs rebound between
        snow mountains of the Sierra

before aurora dew or sun breeze can
clean up the blood. A small bird of paper
        in the lungs declares

that the hour of kisses has not arrived.

Federico García Lorca

No
the moon is you, Federico.
She was your child, lover, death. No one could
save you. They lied to Rosales. Falla came
too late. They plugged an extra bullet in your ass
for being a gay writer who liked strong women, flame
of the dark night of love—*la noche oscura del amor*, the grass
of Andalusia where the tiny monk Saint John soared
from meditation, as a woman, to be one
with God his lord, lover, male whore
and lily moon. Good Federico
dead for the abused moon and sun,
¡NO!

Vicente Aleixandre in His Sevilla, 1952

We meet in April, white April, in spring
in the old bookstore. Luminous in hell.
¡Qué buen caballero! He wears a ring
of gold and poppy red for his Miguel
Hernández and Lorca killed in Franco's realm
of blue religion. No smile like his lips

invented for the *Feria*. In his book,
Sombra del Paradiso, fish move ships
of evening foam like bubbles in a brook
holding up mountains on their open eyes
that see even asleep as they float down
to breed in freedom. Vicente wrote on

the fly leaf, *En el primer día de amistad*,
'On the first day of friendship.' So I come
each year for three decades. The Nobel prize
caused his street name to change from Calle
Velentonia to Calle de Vicente Aleixandre.
Vicente was luminously one. He

suffers from an herpetic eye. It cannot see,
is always in pain and so he writes no more.
'Vicente, don't you dream up poems?' 'Of course,
but when I wake I don't remember.' 'Then
write a volume called, *Unremembered Poems*.'
'Did you', next year my first words. 'I tried, but no.'

He was the last person to speak to Federico
in Madrid—before he boarded the fatal train
to Granada where he was arrested and shot,
He gave Miguel a birthday watch, his first,
but Hernández jumped in a pond. Gone its tick.
This childhood goatherd dispersed new light

of Golden Age verse in his surreal sonnets.
I see Miguel in prison, dying of TB.
I see Vicente mornings and in his night.
One afternoon in Fascist Spain I drove
my motorcycle from our *finca* south of
Granada to our bookshop rendezvous

in Sevilla. In our Phoenician village on
the Moor and Roman coast, Guardias paraded
los rojos, the reds, they caught in the hills,
strapped dead on mules down la *calle*. Lessons.
Guns kill but don't erase the Spanish poets.
Vicente and all those golden birds glow.

Miguel Hernández in Prison Hospital at Alicante

The goatherd boy Miguel Hernández, from
fertile Orihuela that Romans called Orcelis,
is poor, pummeled by his father, autodidact,
the darling of Spanish poets, supreme master
of baroque prosody and connoisseur of moons.
He travels in jammed trains, and at civil war's end,
he is in jail where he contracts his disease.
Like desolate Sylvia Plath, at thirty-one he dies
but he makes paper cutout toys for his newborn
son starving on water and onions while
on his prison cot he coughs up tubercular
liquids that mix with jumbles of roaches
he draws as hungry comrades. Miguel is
the jeweler of shade and love, of light and wheat,
the child of the dark night of the soul
and of the surreal sun that soles his shoes.

Osip Mandelstam and the Kremlin Mountaineer

You said his thick fingers were fatty worms,
His moustache huge laughing cockroaches,
And you caught him relishing an execution
The way a gourmet rolls a berry on his tongue.
Can you blame Stalin for sending you
Into hell? The train to Vorenezh
Was a lovely old icon compared to the transit
Wagon that meandered with its insane,
Sometimes lucid, prisoner who wrote
Pleas for money and warm clothes on a scrap
Of brown paper. Somehow it got through.
Your heart kept graying and then stopped
But the guards in the stars of the Caucasus
Could not permit your death. They made you live

A while. How beautiful the steppes! The lips
Of the moon beamed against your teeth.
In your mouth you perceived snow-blue eyes
Of the heaven over Russia. In the camp
You went insane and slept in a red ice grave.

Miklos Rádnoti in His Overcoat Stuffed with Poems on Postcards to His Wife

Because time is a fiction in the mind
I don't want to die, that is, in July
Or Friday or last year. Farms and haystacks
Are burning today. I, Miklos Rádnoti,
Write you a poem on a postcard. Darling,
I say to myself I won't lie down. The ox
Drools blood. The shepherd girl is an orphan
When the troops stray over the wheat fields.
Wife, after they beat me to death, look through
My trench coat, in the roadside grave, for poems.

Maybe in two years, by 1946,
You will find our bodies. Today all over
Hungary and Poland I am dying. In tavernas
I am already forgotten. How could the smell
of my hair linger? I hid in cellars too,
Smoked in darkness, kissed kisses of the taste
of blackberries. When peace comes I won't be
At the Writers Club. Angels drink artillery.
Peasants drift among fleas, among worms. Wife,
The poems are time's wings. Spread them darkly.

Love Song of Robert Desnos to Youki, 1945

Theresienstadt

Yes, I am rarefied like wires that tie sunflowers around winter clouds
And feverish like the heat under mushrooms
When the forest around a Normandy village
Is smoking with a shipwreck below the eyelids of wild boars,
And still three days away from death in Theresienstadt
I stay alive because I dream you fiercely,
I dream you through the shade of carbon bayonets,
Through hills of stolen gold teeth and that wooden platform
from which our friends are hanged notoriously
                    in public, just for us,
And although my typhus spares me only these hours
to send you a message through a Polish student,
I go on dreaming you as if my brain were made of marvelous steel
                                                                arms
Which hold you and are held by you.

Think, I once said you were a herd of oxen
Remote from me, stopping indifferent,
And you couldn't love me
Even if I stepped through my passions out of the world
                    into greater passions
And became a scholar of love, a diamond-eyed pedant
Footnoting my madness around a table of stars.
But then I hadn't had you, nor you me, and I hadn't had you gone,
As this evil camp has made us gone—or so they thought.
And I am too weary now from camp fever to be anywhere
                    but with you.

I have dreamt you in the mornings when the sun forgot
                    it was a flower
With a duty to feed us its aloof and imperishable beauty.
I have dreamt you at dusk
When airplanes dropped like sugar into coffee, spreading hope
                    to the shackled.
And tonight I dream you, since I love you,

And even my blood, which is reluctant to dance through silk
on its amazing adolescent merry-go-round
for I have run out of francs to drop in it),
My blood still whistles to you. Do you hear me?

I hear you fiercely and love you and quietly in the night
Though sun be weak and too slow to arrange with nightingales
        and dawn
To hurry here bright with your face,
To carry your eyes, your throat to this now free camp
And reach me in time in my burning shade.

Streets Around the Sorbonne, 1948

        The bed is bare. A red
torn blanket below a bulb of maybe thirty watts
        if I can count right,
sputtering high on the ceiling, winking at my wrinkled underwear
        dripping slowly onto the edge
        of the sink. I dress and go out.

        The morning, a sun in her
ragged sock, I walk to my tough philosophy class
        on Auguste Compte. I say nothing
but enjoy the fierce flashing debates between students
        and the good prof Monsieur La Porte.
        One day I arrive. The professor

        had fallen dead. Scrawled
on a piece of bleak paper gleefully tacked to the door,
        a notice: La Porte est fermée.
A Spanish friend sees me let down and gives me a rare book
        of the surrealist Aleixandre,
        Swords like lips that one day

will guide me to a door in Madrid.
We chat about Hernández, his light, his death in prison
Returning home I scurry along
the somber rue de Prince, a little hotel where the prince
Verlaine one good evening lay down,
sloshed and dead on the floor.

Paul Eluard Reading at the Sorbonne, 1948

There in the mob in front of the Sorbonne,
I had disgusting manners. A cop in black
fixed his severe blue gaze on me
and asked and not gracelessly to keep moving.
I answered by stepping on his leather foot.
The flic pulled back wounded, yelping: *Monsieur!*
Misery. I was a real pig. I see his cape.
From '48 I still hold onto that memory

as if I had pissed on holy France.
Faith inside the room for the *Gathering
of Intellectuals Against Fascism*
burned, and Louis Aragon directed.
Seated on the stage next to Paul Eluard,
a priest, rifle on his knees, was listening.
Eluard read the names of miners killed
in a coal strike. Silence. The priest yelled,
If we must fight we shall fight, and then
he leapt to his feet raising his rifle to the ceiling.
Picasso and the Pope urged celebrated Eluard to stop
the deaths. Eluard: 'We must take
one step backward to go two steps forward,' sang
the poet as the hangman killed.

(Soon Eluard in Greece lending support
  to those who *kill for peace*), and he marched,
flowers and comrades, streets of Prague,
  during the terror hangings of his Paris
friend Kalandra the surrealist poet and
  Horakova first Czech woman in parliament.

The poet on the stage at the Sorbonne,
  tired and handsome, had composed
his famous war poem Liberté. He wrote, *Only
  my pain is my property*. An azure fire
lived in his room. A peach in China
  imagined a kiss, an orange of intimate skin.
On only one night I saw him. Happiness lasts.
  In his hand he carried the cheek of the moon
melting in the breasts of blue love.
  Amiable he surged and left, his eyes open.

Tristan Tzara, the Sad Gentleman

We walk along the Seine, not far from 5 rue
    de Lille, where Tzara lives,
the approximate man. We are stepping on dew,
morning is so light. While the clochards sleep,
      the Seine calms not to wake them
and the great Eiffel winks at us. Tristan keeps

his black vest open. Spring makes him more
    gentle than ever though he was
a *Résistance* fighter just a few years before.
I am in *philo* at the Sorbonne. A scamp
    or what a young student is.
We turn on Boule Miche, make our camp

at his corner café, and Sammy Rosenstock,
        as he was in Moinesti,
his Moldavian town in Romania, takes
out exquisite editions of his poems. He puts
        them by his black bowler
and our croissants, carefully. Then shuts

his fine leather briefcase. *I am obscure*
        because I invented Dada,
he laments. Tristan Tzara has no cure
for history. To me the sorrows of his fame
        startle. Courage, wildness.
Now *Sadness in the Country*, his new name,

mocks the impeccable French gentleman,
        so kind to me. He is right.
Whimsy makes and unmakes him Tristan
or Orpheus in his sparkling tongues. The first
        writer I know, he fifty-three,
I the scamp am startled to watch

the torment of the candid man. At ease
        again under our Paris tent,
I have no way to guess an ecstasy of peace
that slid in below the torment when he,
        or a Celan or any exile
drowning in the Seine in obscenity

of madness, forgot the *merde* and wrote
        with élan and *rêve*. Sad
gentleman, you'll take the painted ferry boat
down into the poet sea below your grave
        at Montmartre. It's lovely
how you leap from books and grossly misbehave.

Camus and a Bulbous Plane Tree, January 4, 1960

A whim of fate gives or takes. Often I think
of one letter, in a small calligraphic hand,
       from Albert Camus

a week before he put his return train ticket
stub in his pocket and rode back to Paris
       with Michel Gallimard,

his publisher, in a Facel Vega speed car.
I got his letter about Antonio Machado,
       and also Lorca,

on the day I read in Le Monde about that trip.
Gallimard was at the wheel, racing on a narrow
       tree-lined French

grande route of la douce France, when he lost control
and smashed head-on into a bulbous plane tree
       crowding the road.

Both died. Camus only forty-six. The sweet
austere prince left undone his life, which was
       never absurd.

Marina Tsvetayeva and Her Ship of Being Sailing Even Now in Darkness

Strangely, Marina found her light
and death too early, and she left,
a hounded maid. Trains flowed at night
carting her exile and the theft
of her laughing, staccato knife
of words. Daughter of Moscow, who
hanged from her Russian rope, a wife
beyond the suburbs, floating to
her ship of death. Her ways are clear:
she stares from an Egyptian crypt
with guardian jackals. Her typescript
in braille illuminates a Peking
Man hunting deer. Her ship of being
is out of light, yet always near.

Paul Celan in His Paris, 1970

You always talk to friends and sing for strangers
In one or two of your seven languages
but your murdered parents are always in your mind
in your Paris atelier. Confusion of butterflies.
In a letter from your mother and her white poplars,
That passionate woman of the book

was reading in Bukavina, kneeling among the almond trees
and wheat sloping green like dandelions.
You tried to get your parents to hide or escape.
Your mother Fritzi's hair was blue before the dawn,
She who lived in the camp with killer blue eyes
Until on one milky afternoon of orgy and three violins

She dropped when lead explored her blond Jewish nape.
Death placed stones on her eyelids.
Now at the hour of your triumph and un-triumph,
Your poems lyrically invent German and grow cleaner
Until they are pure calligraphy.
German critics honor you with the Geog Büchner Prize.
Now they attack you viciously.

The knife of guilt and madness wakes.
Your haggard flesh circles your young photograph.
Mom Fritzi raised money for the Spanish Republic.
The dismal Shoah cages you forever in *Die Todesfuge*,
'The Death Fugue', your Johann Sebastian Bach

dancing on a cosmic oven. You always talk to friends
and sing for strangers in one or two of your seven languages.
While the Seine swallows the tears of its small waves,
You wait until the clochards are asleep.
Then walk past their dreaming bodies
And drown in small waves of the white river of night.

Louis MacNeice at his Parthenon and in a Mineshaft

Louis spends an afternoon when he is thirty-one
                with don Antonio in Barcelona just
before Franco and his blue troops pour in
and the loyalists flee to France. Machado smokes
                nonstop, ashes falling on his suit,
unconcerned. Bad cold and lungs, he almost chokes

on phlegm, and works every way he can to save
                remnants of the Republic. 1939,
the catastrophe. Louis the black Irish handsome rave
of English poetry comes to Athens, 1949,
                its savage civil war winding down.
Near our bullet-pocked house the alleys are a mine

of amputees on crutches strolling with worry beads
        past lamb spits turning in small-shop
windows on their way to Omonia Square that leads
straight ahead to the domineering Acropolis.
Louis calls me, inviting me for tea
at his apartment. We chat and then in young bliss

we head for the marble canopy shining on Earth
        with its broken temple arms hugging
the sun, even in winter. Louis beats my birth
by twenty years. For me at twenty-one he's the first
        English-speaking poet I know. We spend
two years in Greece. Louis the Greek scholar says,

'Where's the way up to the fucking temple?' We climb
        the mountain slope. No one around.
Louis trips, cracking his forehead on a sublime
stray Pentelic fragment. Then bounds up, handkerchief
        full of blood, and says triumphantly,
'My first day at the Parthenon and on her cliff

I've mixed my blood with marble.' Louis is low-keyed
        most of the time, except when gossiping
about 'his group of four moderns'. Dreamy tall reed
of gentleness, I'd say. He finds mystery in Crete,
        in Byzantine song. His newspaper self
turns almost mystic. In London, back on his beat

at the BBC, he's doing a documentary on coal mines
        and insists on descending into the shaft.
He freezes, pays no heed, catches cold that combines
with smog to be pneumonia. The young poet's dead.
        Like his friend don Antonio whose lungs
give out, Louis' heart is always dangling from a thread.

Fire Song of Theodore Roethke

I call myself the dancing bear, and though
I'm big and blazing with a bleak desire
To lindy with a beauty—not some crow—
My truth, my skip through hell, is a gray fire
Jakob Böhme saw in a pewter plate,
A dish of sunlight serving up my fate.

That wretched cobbler of philosophy
Gave me abysses and auroras too.
I swing between a mad felicity
And gobs of reverend gloom, the holy glue
That holds my squirming soul in one dark shade.
Each night I sew up holes, but I'm afraid.

Be close to me. I'm sick and shy and try
To dance my arrogance. A man's a bag
Of miracles that cynics call a lie,
Yet if I can't turn ashes or a rag
Into a rose, I might as well lie down
In a Long Island swimming pool and drown.

Dear sweet Beatrice, since Dante found your name
I stole you for my bride. You stole me with
Your swaying bones and we became one same
Slow rising butterfly. We are the myth
Repenting from a dream of solitude.
I dwell there, fat with you and sweetly lewd.

Be kind. I want to live. I try to live.
While egrets whiten banks along the Nile,
Its sewers nourish me, a fugitive
From calm. I wear a pearl (spat by a crocodile)
Under my shirt. It brought me you and day
When all hope drained into mere boring clay.

Under my shirt I am like all of us,
A nakedness that craves eternity.
Sometimes I sing or groan; I make a fuss,
Am caged a while until I learn to be
Easy again with you. Lord, let that flame
of horror bleach a bit, and I'll be tame.

I, Dylan Thomas in New York Where I Read and Plan, Drink and Depart

In my craft or sullen art
Exercised in the still night
Like Lorca off to Granada,
His fatal last evening in Madrid,
I shall pass the grave winter
With you Igor Stravinsky
In hot cool California
Where you built our opera room
For you to compose and me
To libretto our tale of coal mine

And heron-white priested Wales
where the autumnal gales
Punish the hair of lovers
Rocking astonished thighs hugging
Their moons in maddened night.
You, Moscow's discordant note
And my ruffian word will mix
And toss opera to the heavens.
Alas, my hunger for smooching,
My cunning tongue and booze,

And that tank of gin in the black
Cruel night has hurled this glum
Diabetic fool out of his run
On babbling Paradise lands,
And dumb death is my dominion.
So I wake in Hell where poets
Hang hat and soul. I commend
My dream to you from this
Now hollow weakling brain,
But when we both will lie below

I'll jackhammer this Jack back
To you in a tunnel under fat
Oblivious sod. I shall come
At last to our studio room
That sparkles in eternity.
There you will turn my word
Into leaping Welsh Firebirds.
Our tale will soar from fellow worm
Out to stun the Milky Way
And curve the cosmos in song.

Richard Wilbur in Bed

My life is not quite nightmare yet I know
    The misery of a Syrian saint
Roughly strapped to a rock, watching a crow
    Float in complaint
While he the priest of God remains awake,
Full eyed in darkness like the lidless snake.

I've asked the kind assassin sleep to blow
    My brains out so this brooding night
Will wander me to dream, let me forget, or go
    Wholly from light

Below dream's cinema, to seek release
From Plato's deadly charm, and glance at peace.

Some call me prince. It's not a compliment.
     I laugh because while they were home
Or pilots in their khaki planes, my tent
          Was mud, raw loam
My bed, and I a soldier asking flies
And God to damn an SS captain's eyes.

They also mock my passion—those academics
          Who praise my grace and alchemy
And *le mot juste*. It's true I shun polemics,
          Winter by the sea
And keep my meters chaste, yet I recall
The evening Kennedy was killed, that fall

Of Adam and my fractured heart. In flame
          I tore apart the wooden door
Of my small village church, and without shame
          I prayed before
A God I scarcely knew. Was I insane,
Holy? My violence calmed the hurricane

Of mad bewilderment drowning my mind.
          That mind, so elegantly rhymed
And cadenced is a world of things refined,
          But I have climbed
          Through Job's despair, and now in brilliant gloom
I greet old nightmare in a sleepless room.

4 Poems on Ruth Stone

FROM LONDON HORROR
TO A SELECT NEW ENGLAND CAMPUS

January–June 1960

Walter and I spend our last summer in Vermont
before the barge of eternity. We choose a high plateau
for our home. Visitors drop by like foxes. We feed them
as Tang dynasty Wang Wei feeds roaming scholar monks
in Deep South Mountain till they tramp off at daybreak.

We are forever honeymooners. Walter is prince
of savoir faire. I just bought the old clapboard house
and now our big mailbox reads, Walter B. Stone.
Vacation time I meticulously rework lines
of nostalgia and dancing hills for *Iridescence.*

Walter sends my book to Harcourt Brace;
the editor says he loves it, but NOT FOR US.
Walter explodes, 'How dare you love Ruth's poems
and not publish her?' The editor surrenders.
Soon we sail to London town. After a weekend

wandering Cambridge, comes horror. The bell rings.
*The gendarme came to tell me you had hanged yourself
on the door of a rented room.* You hung like a bathrobe in Soho.
I am alone in London town with three young daughters.
Walter's salary at Vassar is frozen. I must survive.

Would *The New Yorker* publish a story again?
I write my confidant Richard Wilbur, who finds me
a job at Wesleyan University Press, and I join the avant-garde.
One snowed-in evening John Cage plays us 4 minutes
and thirty-five seconds of Alpine silence, loose waters in Wilbur's

baroque wall-fountain collapse, Lillian Hellman's red hat floats
like a turtledove over the steeple where Lowell and Frost
play dominoes, and James Wright reads his first poems
to rumbling applause. Though Walter and I have never read
together, for our grand debut we'll choose another galaxy.

RUTH STONE ON HER COLD MOUNTAIN

She lives in clouds on her cold mountain in
Vermont. Only Wang Wei has walked the mist
beyond her cottage—solitary inn
of winds snowing down from the Gap, a fist
of ice punishing deer up on the rim
against the stars. Ruth and the deer don't care.
They don't eat much in winter. But the hymn
she scribbles on a Kroger bag takes her
back to a day in London where a hang-
ing spouse allied her to a Chinese monk,
who sang for decades in her ribs. The pipes
are cracked yet flame grins through the owls. A long
murder made her nun of wind and windpipes,
laughing with ice and enemy of junk.

TWILIGHT

When twilight enters my eyes
the dawn window is almost black.
I walk in the darkness
and find the woodpile in the snow.
Keeping fire in the library helps
to calm the hermitage of loneliness.

THE PASSION

January 22, 2012

Like Lorca,
you who wrote
so passionately
about a death
and a life
are suddenly
upended
by a death.

The moon slips
a blanket on you,
Obits note
your silence,
and deer report
a million
blue coconuts
exploding in Java.

Lucien Stryk (1924–2013)

Lucien Stryk, my classmate at the Sorbonne,
was with marines who stormed Guadalcanal,
but even then he wouldn't hold a gun,
a pacifist soldier in battle. Pal
Lucien in all our cities was the pro
who published poems in *Poetry* as Karl
Shapiro did from New Guinea. Rimbaud
was our hero. His hotel with pink pearl
doorknobs—was near our school. l'Hotel Cluny.
Rimbaud and Verlaine shared a bed, and there
they wrote and fought, but we were just loony,
strolling London and Manhattan, flaneurs
from Paris with our heads lost in Japan
and China. At our last meal we shared a flan.

With Bei Dao and His Painter Friend in a Place Halfway down a Hutong in South Beijing, 1984

Last night Bei Dao and a young painter and I are shivering
in an artist's room in Beijing's coldest December in twenty years.
I warm up by drinking hot water.
The painter goes out for wine so we can be Persian
and mix alcoholic dream with our smoke.
In this city of hidden artists
we all pontificate and are profound.
Listening to Bei Dao so many dynasties patient,
hearing a scratchy Beethoven sonata tape he puts on for me,
I am honored and restored by our elegant poverty,
by books and us conspiring and huddling on the cold floor.
Bei Dao braves those years of writing for 'Freedom Wall'
and enjoys wide readership by the Secret Police.

Ginsberg and Kerouac

And yet this great wink of eternity
Hart Crane, 'Voyages II'

Ginsberg and Kerouac have time to browse
the globe, and days and nights are infinite
to smoke, to meditate, to fuck, to dowse
their brains with alcohol and drugs. They fit
the Milky Way into a chocolate drink
and chug the Daoist cosmos for a thrill.
They're fun and love. They are unique. They blink
and rainbow kites float them to their fill
of Paradise. On earth Allen is sweet
and learned. Jacques is French nobility.
Jack conks out young, reading Chekhov. He throws
up blood. His last words *Holy shit!* He bows
his head. Allen's very sick. Time is Beat,
and yet this great wink of humanity.

Carolyn Kizer and the Gang

It's so quiet tonight
I can hear the angels breathing.
Our hands are transparent
As veined as autumn leaves.
I rest in their arms
And sense the mist rising.

'In the Night', Carolyn Kizer

Let there be light! On my desk, halogen
So my eye-and-a half has light to read
Writers my age. Time is drowning our men
And women poets. Irish Galway is dead.

No light for Merwin who moves in blind dream,
Bly is dementia mad. Cancer ripped away
James Wright, the wild kid on the block. I seem
A lingering ghost when even Strand's gone. 'Hey

Mark', 'Hey Jude, don't let us down.' Shove a cork
In time for flooding Ruth Stone's snowfields. What?
Are you not here, Carolyn? In New York,
After midnight in this Dutch town we put

The moon to sleep and we stroll, stroll, and float
A Persian rug woven by nightingales
And leopards over brownstones to a boat
On Swan Pond by the Zoo before a pale

Dawn wakes brownstones and temples housing Job.
Is Kizer gone? I walk up hills and see
Blind violet stars staring down on our globe.
Carolyn giggles from eternity.

Mark Strand, Lone Sailor (1934–2014)

My parents rise out of their thrones
into the milky rooms of clouds. How can I sing?
Time tells me what I am. I change and I am the same.
I empty myself of my life and my life remains.

'The Remains' – Mark Strand

I like to call Mark Strand Mark Twain.
They both are wry and love to laugh.
Strand is a spinning weathervane
arrowing both you and a daff-
y Mark, the tall and skeptical chief
striding through continents for word
and Hopper paintings. He's the thief
of love, a gallant pirate bird
picking up careful seed to feed
each act of penmanship. I fear
the news is true. Mark has set sail.
Since our twenties we've watched the whale
of time scatter verbal seaweed.
Mark has entered his dark harbor.

Gerald Stern, the Star

Jerry is our Dog Star poet whose chat equals his verse
like soldier poet Archilochos from Paros and blind Borges
mapping his secret labyrinth.
He bats his laughing cosmos with his boxer's eye.
This hummingbird from Hell's Kitchen or Pittsburg,
this Castilian pícaro Lazarillo de Tormes, was born in three riverbeds.
Señor Jeremiah Stern, the divine comedian,
tells tenebrous tales from Paris and Hoboken to Prague,
and cracks our ribs with gallows humor in Vienna
when in a trolley car his foot strays in the aisle

and a Kraut bangs it, curses him, and Herr Stern stands up and yells:
Ich bin ein Jude, und ich werde Sie alle ermoden.
'I am a Jew and I'll murder all of you'
and seven terrified skinheads jump out of the streetcar.

Oh, the Chinese have silver chopsticks when they are rich.
Jerry has a cane of gold so fine it disappears in light.
Monsieur Stern is el Caballero de la Triste Figura,
Knight of the Sad Countenance intimidating windmills and
                                                    blowhards.
He is Dog Star in cold night when blackberries ripen.
He is hilarious Herr Franz Kafka playing poker with Puerto Rican
                                                    pals
to whom he supplies Havana cigars.

In his Point Richmond room on Railroad Street,
he overhears the freight boxcars   couple-fuck, couple-fuck
all night below the voyeur moon.
He is Signor Geraldo Stella di Roma with Waterman pen
composing his white novella.
In le Quartier Latin he hangs his poésie on grand banners for the
                                                    world horizon
from the balcony of his red-rug atelier on rue Saint Julien Le Pauvre.
His closet room has no hot water
which helps this brave upstart from Ukraine/Poland Pittsburg
suffer for divine art.
This young vagabond troubadour hears our chant:
'The Last Time We Saw Jerry',
and his Cracker Jack box harmonica responds:
'He is tramping out the vintage where the grapes of wrath are stored.'

Bonsoir, rossingnol béni, Good evening, blessed nightingale.

Talking with James Wright

James, I could be dead too—we each chose
　　to come up to earth

in the same year, yet you dropped early
　　into the ground under

New York. I see you always at the beginning.
　　You were young, chanted poems

like a rabbi showing off dark truth, which grew
　　huge in the tavern.

Now you are caught in darkness and pulsation.
　　I hear us three decades ago,

dreaming loud in a New England village
　　about Peru, Spain, their poets.

A wild man in proper dress, you drank too much.
　　Over the beers in bad light,

you quoted Vallejo,—'I don't feel like staying alive,
　　heart.' What a lie! Even while

you lie in the hospital, you cannot believe
　　such rubbish. You have better

plans for letting your body follow you, sit you
　　on top of sunlight

transparent like a line of Du Fu blossoming
　　by the Ohio River;

hide you in a gold corn grain. In your bed even
　　after they cut out your tongue

down to its cancerous root, you scrawl poems
on a small lined pad.

Your last word persists intensely like a blossom,
'I shall not be overcome.'

Let's go back with Annie for a meal and drinks
at your East Side flat.

Mary Ellen Solt Sprinkles Salt on the Firmament

She hangs a word in space   It lingers as a black hole
racing to the ends of the
                              universe
where good poets juggle and ballyhoo dexterity
not to tumble away into
o b l i v i o n
Mary Ellen Solt rescues her orphans' weeping word
to reveal to its sixty invisible
syllables
She paints marigolds & the dissonance of childbirth

Solt is our Igor Stravinsky innovator of world poetry
She hides in the New Jersey beard of William Carlitos Williams
She sings sings sings and her orphans sing

Blake
Blake
Blake

Professor Solt wears a chessboard Polish robe
                                          and polished salt
tickling the rump of eternity

Mary Ellen Bottom is her maiden name until her spouse
Leo (the Sun Lion) Solt salts her free of school mockery
Hers is a salad of modesty and know-how
generating bonfires in   Scotland
      Brazil
      Berlin
      Indiana
      Paris
with volcanic
     Forsythias
        tender as concrete

Experimental Lady Mary learns to shape sayings
from her sojourn amid the statues of Easter Island
where she flourishes her bold geometry in verse

Our artist and Kyrios EUCLID the Nile geometer
regularly pow wow over delicious red
in the Mouseion garden in their Alexandria
by the grand Pharos Lighthouse that wakes black seas

Our Lady of the Flowers creases paper into music hall
dancing mimes as she pricks sages into roaring
    !¡!¡ Silence !¡!¡
Married merry Mary Ellen
sits as the hermit in her mansion drawing poesy
or invents her Voltaire garden with lyrical blooms
and she never weeps except for Leo   Then with authority
the planet Cancer strikes her **SUN**   He is unwilling
to let go   The English historian Leo dies in her arms

Let no god ignore Solt's wild crab and dandelion drawings
and her journalistic flare for capturing the murders
of King and Kennedys and eternal wars eternal wars
in poster **broadside** verse for cowboys and dictators
to post upon their withered psyches

Consider Solt
who specializes in hanging words
Each phoneme is a glory land cosmos on paper
You are so jolly in the Cartier Latin
when you attend the *Lycée Louis le Grand*
            with the young maître Charles Baudelaire
already among the cursed the radical *maudits* Next door
in College de France Bergson dazzles his philosophy
of transcendence like wheat stars in orange mustaches
He gives all time at once to Proust and Woolf

but poetry knows that

YOU TWO

Spleen Charles and genial Marie Ellen
            are cooking up deep Revolution
I hear you both intone in cane fields of candor and pathos :
Entends, ma chère, entends la douce nuit qui marche
'Hear, my love, hear the soft night walking'

When after years the snow lion paws of dementia
fashion her last 'little sounds' (true sonnets) in a vast
plain of rain (like songster Apollinaire's *Il pleut*) :
    rainrainrainrainrainrainrainrainrainrainrainrain
    rainrainrainrainrainrainrainrainrainrainrainrain
    rainrainrainrainrainrainrainrainrainrainrainrain)
Dame Mary puts on her black fedora   grabs a hoe
and shovel and shuffles off into memoryville

from
Stickball on 88ᵗʰ Street

Lucy Thibodeau

My first memory of life is
you holding me on steps outside
    a hospital where they
    snipped out my tonsils.
Maybe I am two. We are
already engaged and go steady till
    I am five. Overhead,
    a NY cement sky
more like a photo than a
memory. I am so in love
    with you! Mother is
    jealous and you won't
let her come near. When you
marry the doorman Jimmy and leave
    and have your own
    child (who never learns
to walk), I feel bleak. All
I know for sure is how
    good when Jimmy dumps
    you (I am ten)
and we fix it for me
to come daily to your place
    for lunch between classes.
    I run up the
tenement stairs to the smell of
soup. I kiss a French beauty
    and we talk like
    old times. Now the
adventure will last for life (I
think) and never see you again.
    In the fall my
    sister writes that you
have aged, are thin, are spirited
as always. I think of you
    only a few times
    a year. You formed
me perhaps and time unformed the

work. When you kissed me, what
did you think? Were
mountains infinitely tall? Was
the day just one soup
of 10,000 splendid vermicelli soups
for the elegant court
of our futurity? Did
you know you would ever get
skinny and die? Other women I
have loved disappeared too.
They form you. You
touch them and go away. You
held me for five years, Lucy.
What luck to have
known you, a beauty,
and then you fled for 100
years into the snow to live
in poverty with your
sisters. We come, we
go. It is not different from
death. Thanks for coming to
the window each noon
to look for me
down the stairwell, for not fooling
yourself about how we had to
fail, about how good
we were, how like
insects, cities, and firmaments, we appear
and flare and fall apart. In
that Maine village with
your wheelchair son, I
am outside the house on the
Auburn hill, looking in, completely dumb.

The Building

Babe Ruth lives on the other
side of the court. His brother-in-law
jumped from the 18th
story into the handball
area where we play until tenants
get angry. I heard the thump
when I was in
bed. The Babe gave
me a baseball diploma. The same
elevatorman, Joe, who slapped me for
not being nice to
Jerry (it wasn't true)
took me upstairs to the Babe's
for the photo in the *Daily News*.
Sunday afternoons we hear
Father Coughlin and Hitler
live, shrieking on the radio. Everyone
hates Hitler. Comes a strike, new
men keep billy clubs
by the doors. I
like the scabs same as Ruddy
and Joe outside to whom we
bring sandwiches. I heard
Ruddy got hit trying
to bust in. They almost broke
his head. It's funny for men
to ride me up
the elevator. I always
run downstairs. They slow me down
as I race for the outside
into the north pole
wind and the gully.
But often I spend the afternoon
in a corner of the elevator,
going up and down
in the tired coffin.
When no one else is riding,

they let me close the brass
gate. I do it
like a grown man.

Marbles

During the marble season we control
89th Street. Cars edge by. Only
cabs use their horns.
Alfred is a big
winner. He's got cigar boxes loaded
with peewees and aggies which he
keeps in a schoolbag
like a banker. I
am sloppier and have never gone
into the business of setting boxes
out in the gutter
for guys to shoot
at the square holes. I hang
a few leather pouches from my
belt and the rest
are crunched in pockets
so I can hardly sit at school.
I make lots of noise when
I run. The art
of shooting from midway
in the street at a single,
between a double, or through a
hole is not luck.
It takes good eyes
and thought. Of course you have
to hit boxes that pay off.
I'm a shooter, and
do okay if the
street isn't warped, but I'm not

an acer. Some guys hit all
    the time or flip
    you for cards and
clean you out. We have trouble
when a car wants to park
    and the doorman makes
    us move. Then Alfred
and I sometimes go to his
house where we drop marbles on
    passing cars from the
    roof. We can hear
Jan Pierce rehearsing by holding an
ear against the elevator shaft door.
    I like to jump from
    the indoor balcony down
to the sofa, and don't really
know why it upsets Mrs. Friedman
    so much. I always
    like to jump or
climb. When I leave Alfred, I
go back to the street where
    it's getting dark. A
    big skinny red-haired kid
is walking by himself. And suddenly
I wrestle him to the ground—
    I don't know why
    I start it. We
roll on the sidewalk a while
and then I get back to
    the marbles where there
    are only a few
boxes still going. It's cold and
the Park wind rips through blue
    light and smashes me,
    gets through my knickers
as I head for the Drive.
I don't use the entrance but
    turn the wild corner
    & climb to my window.

from *Stickball on 88th Street*   133

The Boys in Who Climb the Marble Squares
on the Soldiers and Sailors Monument

Last year one of them got
killed. He fell from the marble
    cylinder into the pocket
    between the columns and
onto the tar. Most of those
dare-devil kids are colored. I got
    up to the eagle.
It is just three
stories to the bird, easy climb,
but it took weeks to get
    myself to do it,
    and I stay there
all afternoon, enjoying my warm nest
terrified to look down. The boys
    who climb the marble
    squares just hop into
my booth and shimmy to the
ledge under the squares. They always
    run around it first,
    shouting dirty words. Then
the real climb. The ones who
look poorest in their undershirts are
    the toughest. They crawl
    up, insects. Very few
make the rim circling round near
the ceiling. Then no place to
    go but to hang
    a while from it,
dangle as from a far wing,
hang all their toughness over the
    ocean of air that
    won't hold them up.

Ice Picks on 93rd Street

I am wandering like a sailor
on the Drive. Eliot told me
    Life had an article
    on how babies are
born, with pictures of women.
I don't suppose I'll see *Life*,
    but oh it's great
    to think about them
slowly. Women. Between their legs is
what I see. Suddenly three ice picks
    are against my ribs.
    It's the Price gang.
Brothers. They've been to a reformatory,
I have a nickel but jam
    it into the lining
    and when they search
me they get nothing. But I'm
like stone, unbreathing, so scared I
    feel like a pickle
    with their spikes inside.
When the Price gang is gone
all those blond heads and pug
    noses seem alike. The
    Irish toughs from Amsterdam!
I don't hate them. I thought
they'd be worse. 'Empty your pockets
    or we'll stick you.'
    I didn't think they
would. But I can't walk there
for weeks, as if the brothers
    are always there, waiting
    to knife me for
cash. Eliot said the girls uptown let
you touch their under-panty hair or
    get in their bed
    if you've money. Now
I'm cocky. I've been held up

with ice picks against a dark wall.
Maybe like the sailors
I'll kiss a girl.

Stickball on 88th Street

I'm not much good at stickball
and the kids are tough. Somehow
        it's my turn. In
        comes the rubber ball
slowly in a dream like a
planet that won't spin. It comes
        close, a blazing milky
        rubber pea. I swing.
Bop! My childhood skids along windows,
dropping fair behind a manhole. I
        race scared, ripping out
        to second, miles away.
I must tag the lamppost first,
get by the toughs, not piss
        in my pants or
        bite my tongue. Why
didn't I dump the marbles when
I got up to bat? They
        rattle in my knickers
        pockets. Second is far
as Maiden Lane. If I slip
I'm out! No one's my friend
        on this block. If
        I make it, I'll
pass semaphore and learn to kip
on the highbar. The boys are
        screaming for me to
        run. For me! I
round second. Two kids are yelling

up the street, after the ball,
    as it bounces toward
    wild yellow taxis thumping
down West End. I fly home
through the mobs of black angels.
    Tonight I'll even snatch
    supper from the dog.
The ball floats home. I'm safe,
standing on the side with guys
    shoving me. I'll never
    get to bat again.

Overnight Train

We go to camp by Pullman
from Grand Central Station. 50 groups
    leave the madhouse
    Sunday. I try to
nap in the luggage hammock, then
go constantly up and down from
    my berth into
    the washroom, which stinks
of steam and smoke, whose cold
and hot faucets are curved like
    the dining car's oversize
    spoons. Amid the clacking
metals, the black porter is bent
asleep. Back in the starched sheets
    and tight tan blanket,
    I hear the wheels
all night, the squeaking, the ponderous
thumping and whiz. As we speed
    I gaze eagerly at
    the darkness. I am
the night. The black firmament starts

on my sheet and goes outward
to planets on the
ceiling 500 miles away.
I draw open the heavy curtain
and watch cows looking at me,
see white clapboard sheds
as upright as gravestones.
My eye is huge and tingles,
holding all those outdoor ghosts and
half moon. Finally, sleep
lies on me. I
watch it come, control it like
the narrow berth-lamp over the window.
Each time I turn
the bulb on, all
becomes a small cell with fire.
I got into sleep, deep into
a time absolutely still
except for the wheels
alertly blazing North. When tiny morning
tapes the fields with amazing sun,
I hear cocks, bells.
The cows are still
giving the yellow meadows a haircut.
I shimmy down & rock toward breakfast.

Street People

Old people sit on benches next
to the subway on upper Broadway
or along the Drive.
At times they talk,
often they put their hands flat
on the arm-rests and gaze for
hours. They seem to

be thinking but their bodies are
not moving. Some are what are
    called refugees. Near Grant's
    Tomb with its lively
stone horse, there's always one old
lady whose face is shaped like
    a Singer sewing machine,
    whose hair is white
grass, who uses her cane to
knock nuts across the octagonal paving
    stones on which both
    squirrels and pigeons circle
her. On a side street I see
. a man in sandwich boards advertising
    sneakers pull his penis
    out and leak next
to the gutter. He has white
stubble on his cheek, fat shoes
    and looks blank when
    I look at him.
I am curiously ashamed. His eyes
scan the buildings, then look down
    as he clears his
    nose. Up by Joan
of Arc, and old guy, round
as a tomato, in a narrow
    store sells pastrami sandwiches
    to us between classes
at 4¢ apiece. 'Who next,
who next', he shouts. I hardly
    recall my mother's mother
    and father. She outlived
him, though her hands were shaking
and we couldn't make the slightest
    noise. When the ambulance
    came last night, its
white chassis swallowed a small stretcher
and the machine sped off. The
    doorman said the super's

from *Stickball on 88th Street* 139

girl died of polio.
I wonder what I'd do if
swimming across Lake Beebee my arms
    tired, if I took
in sky water, drowned
and faded to the bottom and became
the whole world in my head
    and couldn't get back
in time for classes.

The Family

Sometimes I go down to Wall Street
and the office on Maiden Lane.
    We come up out
    of the subway like
birds soaring out of a sewer.
Goldsmiths, Pildes! These stores are cities
    with everything man invented
    in crystal and steel
like Brahms played by Mrs. Friedburg
my piano teacher from Germany. Dad's
    walking with me. NY
    spring sun makes us
feel happy. Suddenly Dad takes off
his felt hat with a curse.
    A pigeon shat on
    its light gray dome.
Till then I didn't know birds
could do that to people. Before
    we go into Schrafts,
    I race ahead to
a lamppost and climb up. He
doesn't mind. I remember they found
    the felt hat on

the roof when he
jumped into the spring sky. Smell
of mint and blueberry twinges in
the air. We're eating
cheese pie. The waitresses
are fat and creamy like the
pie. Up in the office Dad
lends cash to a
black Jewish sailor who
missed his ship. Mom, Dad, and
I subway home with three newspapers.
Tired. Dad alertly reads
The World Telegram. Tonight
we'll all hear *Information Please.* By
morning when I hear father screaming
'You God damn bitch,
you. You God damn
bitch, you', he is furious and
gets out the door. Mother and
I go back into
the rooms. As when
the bird shat on the light
gray dome of Dad's new hat,
I'm surprised. I feel
thin and now alone.

Mother

Mother is calm like our Chinese
rug—and firm like the Tree
of Life a painter
put in the wool.
Her eyes are Maine forest green.
She is real as a painting
and just as constant.

Dad calls her Blondie
and she's unreal as an angel
because she keeps mountains of heaven
    inside her, which I
    know nothing of, and
only Sunday morning when I invade
Mom and dad's room and bounce
    on their bed do
    I rouse her to
shoo me off like a monkey
out of India. But she never
    screams or weeps or
    bellyaches. I listen to
the Green Hornet or read funnies
till supper when she can't get
    me to eat onions.
    She doesn't talk easily
but her word is a temple.
She is good, and never gives
    me hell, yet her
    word is there, unsaid
and strong. It's strange to be
so strong and soft at once:
    a woman. She is
    a mystery to me
like women or God or solid
geometry that I'll know one day
    in high school. She
    loves me I know
because of what I overhear her
say to Blanche or Sadie or
    other friends. Mother is
    clear and deep like
a Chinese print with mist, and
I love her like some cloud
    beyond quiet bamboo mountains
    (far inside the frame).

Bessie

Cousin Bessie is a Red. She
is our only political and poor
    relation. We all like
    Bessie and say she's
a good woman whatever she thinks.
She came from Russia with nothing
    but a pair of
    black galoshes. Dad likes
to take her on when she
comes for Thursday supper (Leah's off)
    and always gets cold
    meals, maybe a pineapple
upside-down cake, if any is left.
We sit down to borscht, horseradish
    and gefilte fish. Bessie
    dumped her husband Max
who fought with the Lincoln Brigade
and lost a finger. 'How's Max?'
    I ask her one
    night. 'That bum?' she
answers. Max studied watchmaking but refused
to eat on anything but newspapers.
    Bessie used to live
    in a Bronx basement
in which the icebox leaked, but
she's downtown now and her feet
    don't hurt so much
    from walking. Bess brims
with love. She loves Stalin and really cares
for workers and all poor people.
    Her kisses are famous:
    huge, noisy and slubbery,
and she's so kind and concerned.
She always asks first about me,
    Billy. I go to
    see her and we
talk politics—my first lessons—but

she warns me not to repeat
all this to my
parents. She's always worked,
worked. Recently she took a few trips
and came back hatted and smiling.
We are her only
relations. Her age is
a mystery and joke at home.
She hasn't called so we go
downtown. Bessie's on the
floor, a week dead.

How the Doorman Lets My Father Come Upstairs Unseen Through a Side Entrance

At twilight the doorman and I
go around the corner to a
door I never saw
that lets my father
in directly to the back stairs.
The cars on the Drive are
sedate, carrying authority from
downtown, uptown. We are
New Yorkers and don't own one.
Where is my father coming from?
A place they have
cars? From the city?
It's the first time he's here,
and no reason for neighbors, who
are strangers, to know.
He is not afraid
but is not beaming. It's funny
to sneak him in like Jews
out of a ghetto
to get food, as

if he were guilty for being
my mother's husband. He is happy
   we make it in,
    as if we went
out on the road and sold
a diamond. I'm up again when
   he goes down white
   iron back steps, by
the boiler room, and up to the
wood-and-brass side door. There are only one
   or two solitary cars
   rolling outside. It is
almost twilight. I kiss my father
before we open the door. He
   steps unshaven into half
   light. Maybe in a
week he'll call from out there,
from miles into the light, and
   we'll meet at the
   zoo or down below.

White Nights

For a few days of adolescent
spring, I am so shy I
   want—walking down Broadway—
   to hide behind myself.
My eyes will break like egg—
make a mess—if a woman looks
   and I must glance
   back. Like a small
grape I gulp these stupid feelings
and late at night ponder the
   ceiling. Do I have
   a soul? Is that

a dream made up on the
toilet when there's nothing to read?
My head is like
a magnifying glass. Words
are big in it, and flash
through it like a loud movie.
I lie back, trying
to spot myself or
any face overhead. Outside a motorcycle
roars. I look inside, plunge down.
Only light! Then lie
for hours in dark.
Out of nervousness I pick away
the crown from my watch. I
saw—and lost—light.
The soul is a
thundering word with its profound O
and infinite L. I start to
let go in whitening
sleep. It is dawn.

Women

Eliot says babies come out of
a woman's stomach through
her legs. He tells
me so one afternoon
as we walk by the river
at nightfall. I've never seen where
a girl pisses from
and think no one
has. If I were a girl
for a few days, I'd look
with a mirror and
find out every secret.

I don't know any girls. They
play jacks and hopscotch, prance around
  on the sidewalk while
  we're in the street.
About five years ago when I
was six—so long ago it's
  hazy—I saw, or
  almost saw, two girls
behind some rocks in the park
pull off their panties on purpose.
  They were kids, too,
  jumping up and down
and yelling. I knew two women
for a short time. Last year
  I walked Sarah Whitehall
  home, and even went
up to her apartment and met
her mother. I liked her. It was
  odd and fun walking
  on the sidewalk with a girl. We
talked about Joe Louis who had
just put Max Schmeling in the
  hospital. We hoped Max
  wouldn't wake up. Sarah
asked me to a party where they
would play spin-the-bottle, post office, and
  strip poker. I went
  but she'd moved away
and all we did was dunk
for apples and yell playing blind-man's-bluff.
  Varda Karni is different,
  She's dark. Her hair
is beautiful. Her parents take her
to many cities in the Middle
  East. I'm good at
  school and tell her
what I know about astronomy and
art. I have a crush. She
  seems to fly in
  from far Fifth Avenue

and Ethical Culture. She has swept
through the Museum of Natural History
    and smiles at me.
    I don't know what
she thinks. A mystery. I give
her a copy of Homer's *Odyssey*
    and one day at
    the door she comes
to bring a big letter and quickly
goes. I take it to the
    blue living room, open two
    sheets of white paper
inside each other, and a third
sheet carefully folded to a small
    square. It is blank
    inside. Not a word,
not even Varda. Eliot says he
knows a lot more about women,
    as we slog home,
    & one day will tell.

The Couch

When Aunt Jane or someone else
stays over, I sleep by myself
    (the guest's with mother)
    on the living room couch.
The big room has a blue
Persian rug, a Bubble Boy done in
    1900 by Mrs. Adams
    our neighbor in Maine,
and fake marble antiques from France
of the 17th century done in
    1810. When I perform
    acrobatics on the rug

I stop and look at the
Bubble Boy looking at me. His hair
is angel gold. He
never finishes the pipe.
I think he's me. Tonight I stay up.
No one tells me about my
body except to eat
quickly, although I'm deeply
curious. In the bathtub my dong
floats and I steer it through
sponges and soap foam
until the last water
drains out and its face lies
on the cold porcelain. Now I'm
on my back. NY
stars and the lights
from Central Park come in through
the Venetian blinds, in the dark
living room. I'm playing
acrobatics with my dong,
playing pinochle quickly. It's a Jack
of Spades looking for a Queen
of Hearts. I seize
and hurt it! It's
climbing up away from me when
it shudders and shoots out something
not piss, the sweetest
pain on the planet.
It drains me and the fury
suddenly stops. I think I've leaked
or broken a piece
of my body. I'm
alarmed and happy. Maybe it's okay.
I say nothing. Late next evening
I can hardly wait
till the next room
is silent. The Bubble Boy is dark
and only those bits of light
from the city sky

shine over the couch
where I try out the secret
game again. With slow fury I
play the same Jack
until I get lost
eagerly in a flooding white sea.
It comes! It goes out almost
as strong. The Queen.
I'm in 100 rooms.

Diving

In Latin class I share a
seat with a boy who stinks
of garlic and piss.
When he talks to
me about two girls he screwed
behind a car in a Brooklyn
parking lot, I almost
pass out. 'We switched',
he tells me. 'We were two
guys, and stuck 'em one
at a time.' In the hall
a fellow asks me if I've
heard of the new diver on
the team, *Barnstoni*, an Italian kid.
They wrote up our
meet in the Stuyvesant
paper, misspelled my name. I practice
every afternoon at the 92nd Y.
Once, when I was
waiting in line to
get to the cage where they
give out locker trays, the lady
told me I was

a snot (though I'd
said nothing). Then through the steam
room with fat men and showers,
and finally the pool
with its piercing haze
of chlorine. I wear a suit,
because I dive. The others do
laps naked—you cut
a second off a
mile, the coach says. I place
my towel on the mosaic steps,
stick my gum behind
my ear, hop up
on the springboard, bounce it twice
and ease into an open pike
one-and-a-half. After a few
warm ups, the coach
comes over to the board. 'And
keep your goddam toes pointed.' I'd
be lost without Saul.
He's got rimmed glasses,
is plump, his operation scar wriggles
over his towel. 'And don't stick
your tongue out when
you take off.' On
touching bottom, I push off automatically
to the side and am up
in no time. Once
I came out too
soon from a two-and-a-half tuck and
slap my forehead on the water.
I wake in the shower room,
my memory gone. I
don't know who I am, how
old, where I am. It takes
a few hours to
be okay. (I had
pushed off to the side as
in any dive, and climbed out.)

from *Stickball on 88th Street* 151

When the team leaves,
   the lanes are free
and I practice alone. Now each
dive is a test of fear
   and form. I dance
to the end, hurdle,
my feet driving forks into mat,
wing up over clouds, toward lamps,
   ice stars, the peak
of aspiration, and float
forever until I break furiously in
a tuck. I seize my shins,
   spinning like a moon
   tumbling to the sea,
and open slowly, gliding a spear
into the surf. I sink deep
   to mosaic blur, bend,
   touch & begin to see.

Quakers

My first contagion of dirty jokes,
pranks, women, peace, poems, civil rights,
   and meditation, I pick
   up at the George
School. Ethical flavor is equal to
the constant smell of breakfast cakes
   and shapes me with
   its omnipresent taste and
guilt. When Bayard Rustin comes to
sing, we slip en masse into
   a dramatic group dream
   of the Underground Railroad
when Quakers secreted the slaves North.
Now they simply want to study

but our school board won't
let Paul Robeson's son
or any negro in—until Rustin
sings. He has opened their eyes.
  In the dorm, my
    farmer roommates keep bushels
of apples under their bunks, seeding
them among us circumspectly, as if
  measuring rainfall. Big Jack
    has an iron plate
in his skull from a tractor
crash. He claims his is eight
  inches when we measure
    our dicks in the
dark. It is raining! Buckets fall
regularly on anyone entering our trap.
  We also drop rubbers
    filled with water on
the night watchman—Bucketballs—as he plods
with his cane and tilting lantern.
  In the darkness boys
    sneak from room to
room. Timothy tries to get me
to jack him off. I refuse.
  I want to play kneesie
    with Betty Ross at
supper, but am shy. I have
written notes to girls hand-carried after
  lights-out. Slowly I learn,
    but never stand up
to talk when the *inner light*
comes. It has not illuminated me.
  In summer in Mexico
    we meditate at dawn
in a primitive village and read William
James aloud before our papaya breakfast.
  We boys in our
    Friends' camp are digging
privies for Indians. I am Guillermo

and fall in love with two
      college women, and will
      go everywhere to find
them. The dream begins, leading me
from lips to lips. They teach
      all kinds of love
      at the George School
(except between bodies in a bed)
and we're told not to hate or kill
      even if they are
      Nazis wiping us out.
The last love (good for life)
I don't know is mine: poems.
      Robert Frost comes to
      chant birches. While the
old man vainly intones his simple
deep verse, I hear Mr. Rustin
      singing like an angel,
      like a black nightingale.

Selling

Father has lost everything: the business,
his wife and children, his wild
      confidence. I'm with him
      for a long summer at
the Greystone Hotel. I have to
study Latin and when we're not
      talking or out selling,
      I follow Julius Caesar
into Gallia and that farthest outpost
where the hairy Britons live. Our
      room faces Broadway, but
      we're high enough not
to hear the noise. The Greystone
has known better days. We say

we don't care. It's
good to be together.
He shows me how to shave
and I practice carefully, imitating his
stroke and the way
he uses his fingers.
He has nothing left from his
company but three valises: mainly straps,
eight fancy gold watches
in modern shapes, some
semiprecious stones and a few
small diamonds. We figure about $500.
Enough to live through
the summer. And then?
What we sell we share for
rent and food. I am thrilled
because I am with
Dad. He's showing me
things, and we often chat through
the night, from bed to bed,
with the deepest confidence.
I adore him, and
he always tells me I'm his
one love. But he is pained
and depressed, though he says
with me he's not.
We take the IRT to Wall
Street and systematically make the rounds
of each jewelry store.
Some of the owners,
old clients, recognize father. He gets
furious, embarrassed, or glad according to
what they say. We
lay the valises with
straps on the counter and Dad
begins to sell. I too add
key information about soft
Swiss leather. If we
sell 2 gold watches and 100

from *Stickball on 88th Street*   155

watchstraps, we can make it through
a week of diners
and the Greystone. If
we have a good day we celebrate
at Starkers or some better place.
Dad shows me how
to read a newspaper
in the subway, folding it correctly.
What will we do when it's
all gone? Yet father
trades a few stones
and buys a diamond with all
he's got left. He sells it
a few days later,
doubling our cash. Now
he brings out the stones first.
On Sundays we boat or go
out to a beach
or watch the seals.
He's thinking of leaving the city.
We make all kinds of plans
at night. I see
him shaving, his face
lathered and sparkling. One late afternoon
we are strolling up Broadway. I'd been
studying Latin words for
hours. The top papers
on the stand read: GERMANS INVADE
POLAND! WORLD WAR! Father's going west
and I must soon
separate again from him
when we have finally found ways
to be free, to keep all
riches in a tiny
velvet cloth, and laugh.
One day in China I dream
of father coming into the room.
He's shaving. He's come
back to talk again.

The Call

I am with you in NY
at a hotel. You're in bad
    shape. Just a year
    ago in Colorado we
all walked with the wirehair bouncing
on the sidewalk. You put in
    a line direct to
    Denver and were to
civilize the world with silver goblets.
You've moved too quickly again. We
    talk about it through
    the night. You've dropped
so low I seem to be
your father now. I speak firmly,
    telling you to resist.
    Why do I speak
this way? Something prods me. Perhaps
that's what you need. But we
    do talk well. You
    know as always I
love you. And I know what
I am to you. I have
    to go back to
    Maine to finish up
the term. I don't like to
leave you. Now I'm the only
    one of us you
    see. We say goodbye
and I promise to see you
soon. Back at school, I hope
    you will pull money
    out of the sky,
you will somehow fight and feel
better. It's finals here and I'm
    cramming. My roommate Bernie
    from Austria tells me
not to worry so much. But

he's pre-med, works like hell too.
The phone rings. Dad.
'Can you come down
right away to NY?' 'You must
be crazy', I say, 'This is
exam week. I'll mess
up the whole term.'
I am angry. I am surprised
that I'm impatient, but something prods
me. 'Please come.' 'Dad,
I can't. Please wait
till I get through finals. Are
you okay?' We talk some, but
I can't remember words.
He's in bad shape.
I shout at his sadness which
is piercing me. 'I'll see you
soon', I say. Click.
The week is a blur
but I'm on the golf course
with Roberto and Hans from Mexico,
first time I've played.
We come back late,
a bit slaphappy after the grind.
'Someone's been trying to reach you
all afternoon.' I call
back. My Dad's assistant
in Colorado. 'Your father left NY
for Mexico. Then he flew here.
He jumped around noon
from the top of
this building. Are you coming
to the funeral?' I leave for
NY. No one else
is going out West
except a business friend Jack who
is loyal although stuck with debts.
They tell me he
folded his topcoat neatly

and put his felt hat alongside
before he swan dived and forgot to
    float back up through
    the warm May air.
There are some silver goblets left
I take with me. I cannot look
    at his face. I
    don't want to remember
anything but my father live. The
air has a mountain clarity. It
    is beautiful there. I
    will not be alive
the same way again, without him.
I can't take that untaken trip
    to NY. He is
    with me even now.

from
Inventing China

The Cave of the Peking Man

Soon after dawn a red dust is in the sky
and old men shadow box

or jog in shorts around the block. Shanghai cabs
are driving on their horns

in the Great Plaza of Heavenly Peace.
The masses in blue trousers

hurry to work. We go west by the Silk Road.
Mirrors float on the paddies,

fields stink of human fertilizer, and hills
of green ink are fragrant

with wild herbs and mist. The ancient cave
is empty. We climb down

and rub our fingers futilely on the wall
where the cranium was stuck.

The Peking Man is gone. He may be in
a marine's footlocker

or at the bottom of the Pacific or in
a Japanese coffee shop.

His forty comrades of the cave have also
split. They stopped breathing

about half a million years ago. The masses
in blue trousers hurry to work

and dig up ancient coffins of an emperor
or greatly raise production

in a rubber shoe or paper factory. We have
been dying for a long time.

After Midnight in the Streets of Beijing

Red dust has fallen for the night
and I should sleep too, but I slip

downstairs, hop across the marble
grade where the chauffeurs hang out,

and suddenly in a city with
only a few eating places

open, the avenue of fans
is an empire of locust trees

where the moon with its cement face
glares on the few creatures moving

below: a tank truck watering
the tar, a lone sweeper, and me.

My feet have swollen from dread
disease or from roaming the Long Wall

but I couldn't care less. I leap-
frog over a big steel trash can.

No one spots me—am almost lost
in the great underground metro

where Beijing is to hide out when
the million Russian troops across

the border let the rockets fly.
I fly like a fire in a bamboo

forest, all alone in empty
China. How lucky I am here

with all these ancient alleys of jade
where three emperors came from

their village to find the apples
of silk. I knock quietly at

a thin door in a dark patio,
walk in happy and disappear.

Sewing Up a Heart During the Cultural Revolution

Shanghai. I smell my fear among the smells
of medicine and patients in the hall.
The nurse ties on my mask, quietly impels
me toward the table, but I hug the wall.
Hard to witness the bloody cut mushroom
of a man's heart. The eyes are open as
he sips a bit of juice, and the perfume
of death drips off a nylon thread which has
repaired the shadow of a soul. His ear
holds one electric needle, quivering.
His eyes call out. I think about crazed Lear
carrying his daughter, drownings off Vietnam,
my coffined mother on the train. All being
is good. The dark and gentle night is sham.

Red Guard Beijing, 1972

Madness is in the air. There is a smell
of progress from the fiery factories and
from *hutongs* and mass toilets. The death bell
of nightingales is heard throughout the land.
I wear my Mao button. At the opera
my comrade from Inner Mongolia informs
me that 'this joint is really jumping!' Ah,

I am a fan. I catch the zeal. Reforms
have unbound ankles, freed the children hidden
in dark mills, cured the deaf. The once Forbidden
City is a museum. I'm at the zoo,
I boat romantically on the snow lake
where once the Summer Palace Empress threw
heads in a well. Red Guards keep death awake.

Snow

Summer collapses like a red flag
and I turn into snow,
a snow mountain with no mountain inside.
Just dark bones needing a new shape.
I face it. Turn into nothing. And must go
to Central Asia to make a new self.
The cadre also judge and exile me to that countryside,
supposing it a punishment.

When I get there, the old paper house is remote.
I am a woodcutter in the mountains
and have a hut. I sing, cook yellow herbs,
and my Han and Dai friends laugh at me.
We drink beer under the moon and hear oil lamps
and panthers.
It is my last voyage.
And when death finally inks me out, I've lost nothing.
That all fell far ago like a red flag.
Only a pear tree that no one can hear is talkative.
Like geese fading over a river over a river,
every illusion is now.

Potted Flowers on an Oil Cloth-Covered Banquet Table in Our University Courtyard

After supper I am talked out. The moon is yellow
and has a forest of stone hands
that keep it from singing.
After drinking sweet wine and digging into Mongolian hotpot,
after euphoria and shaking hands with the cook,
I'm outside the red building in the court with Wang
who reminds the moon
about her old drinking companions, Li Bai and his shadow,
who jumped up to a river of stars.
I'm all talked out. The rusty gate around the compound
drifts in fog like a fisherman lying in his boat,
wandering in a peaceful garden lake
others call the soul. The moon's hands are green.
I've one less day in my life. I leave.
The old school's locked up. No one in the street.
It's only eight and the city's dead,
but a Buddhist flute works up to heaven.
Soon I'll be back in my chair, trying to turn into books.

Trashcart Mule

As I hear my school gate, just another worker on
my Flying Pigeon bicycle, used to dodging death,
sharp in sniffing out coal from dun in drizzling rain,
I pass an unturned trash cart
and brake because its muscle is waiting stiff,
a splattered statue,
garbage hanging on it like rippings from an ancient codicil.
The driver on his knees, sweeping, ordinary
in hurry to amend, ignores the small crowd.
I can't stay to watch
but the incident is perfectly serious. It is a

chronicle of minor calamity
and a test of moderation. I leave the small crowd for duty.
The incident is closed,
no time to see the resolution and clean-up
of the animal and the street,
of the resurrected driver and his patient mule,
eyes bulging yellow with sun,
trash hanging on its black hair like wasted garments
from the mighty emperor Qin Shi Huandi.
Standing half-naked, a mere staring mule,
the beast is more alive
than all the emperor's terra cotta generals and stallions
dug up and exposed to light,
who, from their open tomb at Chang' an,
glare straight ahead in eternal boredom.

On Wangfujing Street near the Beijing Hotel, 1984

In China a brilliant autumn noon.
Rushing shoppers smile.
The good life. Soon lipstick and earrings
will be permitted. At the corner
Uighers in borsalinos and Humphrey Bogart suits
change dollars for *renminbi,*
the people's currency. Slowly passing by
appears a big open raw-wood wagon
pulled by a red truck. The wagon is jammed
with ghastly-faced men and women convicts
in black gowns and cropped hair.
Their heads and eyes are downcast
on their way to the countryside.
On this busy shopping street
with their new colorful department stores
no one looks up at the condemned
who are soon to kneel in a long row.

A pistol will press against the back of each head,
a cadre shout and one shot fired through the brain.
Each family will be billed for the bullet.

Pilgrim Climbing a Holy Mountain

1

The sun and moon float together at daybreak
over the windy summit of Taishan, the Holy Mountain.
I lived one month on Agion Oros, the Holy Mountain
in Greece when her army was mopping up stray guerrillas
hiding behind snow meadows in the forested peninsula.
But not even ghosts of the wild Tartar rebels in the west
were a threat to the Jade Emperor.

2

People climb the most sacred peak in China.
Hundreds of old ladies with bad tiny feet and black velvet hats
pass through the Red Gate
and stop at the first Daoist temple to prostrate
themselves before the local clothed bronze goddess.
They flame a piece of paper before the tiny shoes
on the altar and toss small coins on it
between the candles and incense.

3

Candles and incense now fill the cave where the Theologian
wrote his epic Revelations in Patmos.
For two years John lived on the island, penning Apocalypse
while seven white whale islets circled on the sea harbor
below his white hill village. They kept the hermit monk company.

4

Gales at the summit of Taishan fiercely slap
old men in black padded trousers
and couples next to calligraphed old steles
where they become immortal in the lenses of dinky Sea Gull cameras.
Wind almost blows me off the rock bridge.
The sun and moon kiss their own sides of heaven.
I pass through the seven moon gates,
follow a rocky path where lovers leave bottles,
where a smell of shit is intensified by wind blasts
as I near the mythic top Temple of the Azure Cloud.

5

When I leave Patmos on a small caïque, hugging the bowrail,
the meltemi almost blows us off the helmsman's deck.
Wind ecstatically kicks up on the icon-blue water
            between the islands.
The cave of the Apocalypse is stuck for good in my head
Pilgrim steps of Taishan are already becoming memory
where old women with tiny feet prostrate before
the bronze goddess of the mountain
and porters crazy-eyed balance 90 beers on their pole
            up to the workers' bars,
with Shandong sand-wind beating into my unholy eyes
and the summit circles, swaying under the radar tower
            and sunrise boulders.
I look far below at faint white
spring in the valley. Time freezes. I never descend.

The Great Wall of China

Most of the Long Wall, as the Chinese call it, is a ruin
and almost as old as Plato's beard.
In walking in the north I see it suddenly
crawling into a poplar valley,
flashing through turquoise autumn.
On a hill it has gold rings like the fingers of a god in armor.
It spreads as a great river of stone
against Mongols and Manchus.
It is beautiful as a dazed sunflower, and useless.

Another wall, of equal grandeur, snakes around my hotel
            and university,
snooping outside the huts of strangers in the hutongs
and next to friends in their guarded flats.
It is ugly
and sinister as an informer's notebook.
Often, even in the raw sun battling the haze over polluted cities,
it is invisible,
and like scorpions in shores or rats on their chest
my friends in blue coats fear it.

On rare days when the Secret Long Wall is merely a ruin
sterile and dried up by the moon,
you my closest friends persist in seeing its watchtowers
            and telescopes
as an astrologer sees gold typhoons blowing among planetary rings
On these benign days, I phone you,
but you fear passing through its gate to my room
as if you were still Mongols and Manchus, Tibetans or Uigurs
outside the stone eyes of the dreamt-up dragon.

The wall is heavy, omniscient, everywhere
so your feet are tattooed and turn to stone,
and I am like you—foolish, cowardly, sane and streetwise.
Who can walk against the Great Invisible Wall?

China Songs

1

Chinese half moon, piece of jade,
a bowl of ride to feed the stars,
out in the West you were a gambler,
putting a new face on each night.
Here I take you back to my room
and sit you on my bamboo sheets,
You kiss me. So I wake from
being awake. One day they cut
off my hands and I wasn't even
a guitarist. You kiss me whole.

2

Why do I love you? I wrote you
a secret letter. And you sent
me cinnamon apple pie and words
I had no glasses to read. And soon
we were lovers. Yes, in China,
where love is ancient as lions
sleeping out in persimmon wind.
Will you ever leave me? I knock
on the door of the rain. We run
back into the mist to be alone.

3

Are you really bored? You gaze
at the fruit wagon like a gazelle
in Sinai baffled before a Hebrew
verse carved into the desert hill.
Don't worry. We're all just wise.
You took the train and I met you
on a sunny spring day. Isn't that
everyone's dream? Don't you know
one day we'll descend into
yellow springs and live forever dead?

4

Don't be unhappy. Time is good.
So good each second we are breathing
bread. What's a little despair to
the orange tiles of a long dynasty?
China is more than a plate. My Greek
friend wrote that wherever he goes
the marble wounds him. How lucky
to be ancient! China is a world
of one woodcutter in the mountain.
O hermit, yes thunderously quiet.

5

You're good. This is a good night.
I'm jumping out of my sky because
you're so warm. Don't abandon me.
We slept alone for centuries.
I put on my shirt, took your hand
and fund what sleep alone never
gave me. You. We were born alone
from night into gold. I've waited
all blood long. It's easy. I sing
and gamble, lost in our jade moon.

The Pungent Smell of China

1

Each afternoon I pedal home from work, a ghostly robot
amid slow cycling gangs in dreary Mao caps.
The imperial city is shorn of its city wall Mao tore down.
Women ride with coarse nets draped on their faces
against sandstorms in the massive squares.
I try to skirt around lumps of mule shit. Through a break
in the street wall I make out Fragrant Mountains in the west
sleeping in their violet elephant wrinkles.
The slopes have a wildflower tang, Sunday morning fresh,
as Gobi winds float dust into the city's soft coal haze.

from *Inventing China*   173

2

Beijing is demolishing its smoky wooden rooms.
Cranes with giant beaks and legs migrate out of the marshes
and stride into construction sites,
balling down wretched smelly huts, their door carvings
and crooked iron windows. They step through mud brick alleys
and a rare mansion with orange roofs
yet somehow spare noisy Grand Street of the Gate of the Sun
or herb shops and theaters on Great Barrier Lane
with its old rambling bordello now a silk store.

3

As when a mob of Christian monks clamors outside the house
of the beautiful Hypatia of Alexandria, and stones her to death,
liberating this great city from its last pagan mathematician
        and neo-Platonic philosopher,
so Beijing bids goodbye to the open sewers,
to atrocious stench of outdoor toilets with old men publicly shitting,
to scented rooms of love making, to shadows of bodies
haunting opium dens and sin houses and secret societies,
and, near the Marco Polo statue over the brook,
to the ancient Temple of the White Clouds filled with superstition
        and woodblock books.
And a young monk in loin cloth in his twenty-four hour trance
before a gold Buddha in an unlighted hall,
to the jasmine courtyards and forest of old alleys, and to small
wretched outdoor markets with delicious fruit.
Beijing bids goodbye to the pungent smell of China that is leaving.

from
Life Watch

Daybreak with Jean-Louis Kérouac

Never expected Jack to show. I'm eating supper
with Gregory Corso in a lonely blue Italian joint
in New Haven. He is coming up alone to read

his poems at Wesleyan. Bragging about Jack,
Greg gets mournful, as if Kerouak had spun off
the planet. I say, 'Look, Jack's not a corpse.

He's alive, knocking it out. What kind of shit . . .'
Corso, the straight pin of the gang, lets me have it,
'Ginsberg sleeps with everyone. Allen, poor Allen,

he's just a whore. I'm the only straight dude
who's ever slept with Jack-o'-Lantern. We're tight.'
Corso's proud of being top gun with Kerouac.

Jack stinks out loud with whisky, but off booze
he's really low key, gentle. He's a timid man.
On the weekend, Greg shows. He's come up

from the city with a tired wobbling bum wearing
a black ratty raincoat hugging his ankles,
a black fedora and shades . . . HEY, KEROUAC!

YOU GOTTA BE KIDDING. Drunk as a hog, his feet
made of cotton, Jack's smiling a lot. I ferry him
to Olin Library and present him to Professor Greene,

expert in Christmas carols. Jack asks Greene,
'What are you teaching, sir?' 'Shakespeare,'
responds the patrician teacher. D'yuh like

Shakespeare?' says Jack. 'I love Shakespeare,'
states the professor. Overjoyed, Jack shouts,
'I love Shakespeare too!' And he grabs his new

friend's cheeks and slaps a wild kiss on his lips.
I've read your books,' says Greene. 'I like em.
Where can I take you?' The scholars skip off.

*

In the evening, Corso stuns me. 'Are those tramps
going to beat me up?' 'You're crazy.' But Corso
won't read his poems. He raves about his hero

William Burroughs, whispers a chapter from *Naked Lunch*
and we're transported to jungle rapture and shots
of heroin Burroughs sticks in the ass of a Brazilian boy.

After a discourse on love, Greg and the gang of pals
Jack came up with from New York jams into a side room,
and Jack is sober and describes his dawn climb

up Mount Tamalpais north of the Golden Gate.
Jack is impassioned. 'I climbed Tamalpais.
'I got to the top and beheld daybreak. I saw satori!'

'You saw bullshit!' Corso throws in. 'I saw bullshit',
Jack confesses. He surrenders. A buddy knows I'm nuts
about everything Greek and puts on an LP

of *hassapiko* from Asia Minor dens. Jack tells me,
'Let's dance.' We squat, arms locked, and we're doing
the butcher's dance strict and low until Zen daybreak.

Stopping with John Cage on a Snowy Night

Before I sleep I dream of snow
in bright New England winter. There
snowed-in one night, Cage says: *Let go
of words*. And so we argue till
the dawn, John the fun Buddhist freak
armed with his silent piano, and Bill

the young companion of the lost
magician and his unheard notes.
And then I dream of Robert Frost
reading the *Odyssey* in Greek,
who lets the *Georgics* guide his plow,
this crude farmer of bloom and bleak.

Cage and I scream. Fields are white glow.
Out together, John points at fresh
wordless deer track printed on snow
and waves goodbye. Critics call Frost a boor
and populist, but after lunch
we stroll up to the old man's moor.

These old New England friends of night
now sleep deep yet also tease me
for fearing their world of black light.
Before I sleep I watch a way
to let peace come. It won't and sun
pops in with a gold wordless day.

The Postman in Love

I'm walking the circumference of our island,
carrying the breath of the postman who is young,
        only seventeen,
when he dies inexplicably in the garden
with a love letter pinned under his cap.

Inside my life watch an eye still winks
to see the postman while his corpse hears the bells toll
on the minute from echo mountains.
The old ladies and I eat a big salad of tomato and cucumber
        in olive oil for him,
and the sky opens,
turns mauve and expands unaware of its new desolation.

The mourning doves sing to the young postman
only seventeen years when he fell.
I have no love letter for you pinned on my shirt.
We are lost in our arms inside our whitewashed rooms
        over a ravine of rocks.
We have breezes in our lungs
but I envy the sweetness of the young postman
who sang island songs gravely and died in the garden,
sweaty, with a coarse bag of rosemary and salt
give the forlorn.

Companions of Light

On a dirt road from the island's mountain town
with its round white church and town hall clock
to a lone village now almost abandoned,
I fix my eyes on jasmines hanging over the stone wall
around some interior garden.
                    A crooked arch

shadows and cools the wrinkled eyelids of the cobbled street.
I stop and look at the ashen mountain
and back to holes of grass and a delicious honey blur
        standing everywhere.
The black cloth of mind falls away, and sheep seem to fall
back over the horizon just below the hermitage and Makários,
its one kind lecherous monk, lying in his robes,
chattering to himself on his cot.

Cloudy ships rock like slow whales going nowhere
under a family of clouds
and through the holes in jellied clouds to the optic nerve
the jasmine petals glisten. They are letters of light
now perfectly visible and unreadable to a blind man
whose dead eyes look through gray wrap-around glasses,
who I remember is me,
who through the aqueous nothing in his sockets
imagines that winter is a July afternoon and a dolphin sun
        greater than light.
And this happy face with a black lens behind the iris
(the mad happiness is unreasonable)
smells every color of the floppy white shapes on the wall.

At the Saint James Café in Dirty War Mornings

Often in Buenos Aires during the Dirty War
I am translating sonnets of Jorge Luis Borges
who has an apartment on la calle Maipú
right across the street. Blind he no longer sees the page
but in the unanimous night he repeats his own lines
with the sonority of calm thunder.

Normally we walk to the Saint James Café
on Corrientes to have our breakfast,
his place for a chat about the enigma

of Alice's first word on ascending from the rabbit hole
into which she had tumbled
and then played croquet with a flamingo,
or how his almost fatal fall on the circular stairway
in his building led him to his first story.

On these long mornings we sit with coffee and corn flakes
where the great mirrors show his white collar,
his head and always-gazing disfigured eyes
and his black and impeccable suit.

Feeling His Midnight Arm

Especially after midnight when we walk
around the city, Borges loves to stroll
and spin around his cane and stop to talk
and talk, and never stop; he spends a whole
hour comparing Hopkins to his Milton. No
taxis, another strike, the hospital
once more filled with young *montoneros* who
fight the police and lose and we are full
of midnight books. We move again. This team
of arms. He's blind and eighty and I'm half
his rascal wisdom. All this spoofing in
the night. Then dawn informs us: we must laugh
back to our flats, our night vanished again.
I grieve. Borges's dead eyes are fixed in dream.

In the Beginning

In the beginning the life watches on the wrists of living beings
    measure that turning of time and of now
and twilight and twilight and the blackness.
By daybreak these inhabitants have bodies and consciousness
and see that it is good and they are in time,
and some of
them weep on the ground
and would disappear from time as disappearing dust
    floating out of time,
and they are terrified and eager to form paradise and God
and God tells them to live and God tells them to die
and they are happy and with God
and some are not pleased with God whom they have made,
and some are found and some are lost
and a multitude of lonely inhabitants stand on the earth
    and think of their fragility
and in their loneliness look through telescopes
and in microscopes they look for a sky below their feet.

And while they choke from labors on the heating globe,
straggling through gravity to remain erect,
these lonely inhabitants see the solitary planets of desert,
    ice and terrible gases,
these near dead children in the wilderness of space,
rolling overhead around their mother sun dressed in fire
    and piteously remote.

Only earth is a blue residence with carbon and oxides,
only earth grows a whale and leopard, lily and oak,
only earth holds the multitudes of breathing minds
residing here to eat and defecate and bloom.

Aeneas

In blazing Troy he lifts his father on his back
and they escape over the dawn hills of Ida.
Now after wandering Africa and the sea for seven years,
Aeneas enters the underworld to see his father
whom he embraces but he touches shadow.
His arms find only themselves and his despair.

Yet Virgil is deeply wrong. His creations rebel.
In death the father Anchises is alive and busy,
not merely a ghost of darkness waiting
for his son to descend. He has his own farmlands
and slaves whom he remembers through the son
and the fleet ferrying them all away from Troy,
and there is more than the escape.

There, long before the fires ravage Troy,
the father is walking in his coastal forests,
ordering his foot soldiers to gather wood and weapons
for an early march. And after these early tests of prowess and
adventure,
of warrior and son routing ordinary enemies,
the old phantom of a man, still with all his senses,
recalls his young companion, how he loves his son
so obedient to his own heroic hours,
how the robust Aeneas once carries him to safety
yet then deserts him by remaining up in sunlight.

Blue Tibet is Very High

Blue Tibet is very high. Fog hangs on yellow fields
    of mustard plants.
Hard to breathe
at the top of the world. In far thin air
some leather-faced nomads tramp by in black rags.
Up here in rooms in Lhasa
    the nuns are tortured, the people in terror,
and in ribbon villages the sole monasteries not in rubble
    are ghost cloud mirrors
of packed highland summer snow.
The skinny police are walking in gray cloth bags.
Along the hills, strings of prayer flags flutter in winds,
    defying guns.

Spinoza in the Dutch Ghetto

Smoking his pipe he takes a beer with friends
at a close eating place or back at home
and shop, he grinds the glass to make his ends
meet needs. Lean life. Then drops down to a dome
of Latin thought and pen. Why ask for more?
He trades his work with Leibniz who is keen
as calculus to open every door
and wheel him into Germany to teach
and make him known. The lens grinder has seen
that greater world only in spheres that reach
the end of mind, and all mind plus all sphere
is God for him, a thought that by itself
could set his life on fire. Baruch (the blessed)
calls peace a virtue. He's all sky. No fear.
A Spanish Jew safe on his Lowlands shelf,
a bird on the North Sea, thought is his nest.

Of Julio Who Almost Kills Me

I wonder if I can forgive Julio Cortázar
who conspires and almost crushes me.
He does it by writing a mysterious story
I am reading in a Buenos Aires subway,
standing, rocking a bit in the clanking car.
It is not 'End Game' but a fantastic tale
of two houses and a railroad car with a rider
who never arrives yet is forever a woman waiting
like me in the train, not wanting to look up.
Argentina. Every day during the Dirty War
is better than the next. I've always liked danger
in demoralized lands with autocratic regimes
and the comradeship of persecuted writers.
Here under Perón and his vigilante thugs
in plateless Fords halting at midnight houses
to help an artist disappear, I am excited by
Julio, the Argentine short story magician, and read
lost. As we move around a curve, I lean back,
feeling for the car wall when a middle aged lady
says quietly, *La puerta está abierta* The door is open.
She saves me. Julio is alive, and if he'd killed me
I would have preceded him into shadow land
where I'd have time to read forever, with proper glasses.
I forgive Julio. Grimly, with no one to warn him,
the multiplying white cells will crush him early.
But down there, alert with his shadows, I see him
unwilling to forget his eternal readers. With only
a pencil he dreams up novels and fantastic tales.

When I Die Bury Me with Raw Onions

When I die bury me
with raw onions and garlic
so I can keep healthy,
and a digital phone
to apologize to those
I hurt by dying,
to those I hurt by
having been around.

And don't forget
to call. And if you
have old equipment
and can't get through,
with your learning
stoop on my grave,
dig a small hole
and I'll be waiting
for your whisper.

And through the ceiling
of garlic-smelling earth,
I'll dig back up to air
and press my lips up
to greet the impatient
who love me, whom I love,
whom I leave helpless.

Snow in the Dakotas

This afternoon the Dakotas are shedding snow
again on Badland reservations and bleak hillocks
as I walk in the blizzard like a drunk drinking

spiked wind. The *Coast to Coast Hardware*
is a pleasant shock of heat. In my borrowed boots
I trail trucks and a limping cat and huddle

for a while, looking over a Sermon of the Plain iced
for followers, snow ghosts like me with my codicil
of heavenly words for freezing transcendence.

A shot of Sandman port before I sleep,
a mattress in the Dakotas where my blood asks me
to snore through bedless months (to sleep in my own

sheets is strange). Aliki lies in rhapsodic linen,
on rags of dream. We've had our gifts on earth.
Standby. I've flown here for a freezing teacher

unable to take food, my daughter near death.
In dim Dakota I follow a pickup home, a white night,
a star in my throat, and gales of snow and snow.

Rooftop

If when my father climbed the iron stair,
folded his coat and neatly set his hat
on top, and neared the guard wall to the air
of Colorado spring, and squinting at
a circle in the street that would bring sleep,
he saw a child or heard a crazy fight
over a baseball card, or if his leap

would have smashed me posted under his flight
plan, if a girl had cried, if a Ford truck
had howled up to his ears, then the squat wall
would have spun him around, me at his side,
hugging him down the steps. He'd never fall.
I tried to come on a red-eye plane stuck
in storms, which hit the tar just as he died.

Dawn Café

I sleep and already live tomorrow. Must be
Monday. No, it's a beautiful negligent Sunday
      morning

and I dance with God, a beautiful woman
who tells me mouth to mouth in my soul
      the banal

secrets of my confusion and why
I can't sleep, why I feel forced
      to get up

from sleep to speak to you in the black,
in the hours before the dawn café
      that saves me

undoubtedly. I kid myself. I kiss
the mouth of God. She is soft and doesn't
      blame me

for dying without hope. She assures me
her presence isn't necessary
      and I love her,

devastated by her remoteness. I'm cold.
Winter lies remorseless on my knees. Warm
    she is smiling.

The Shtetl Ghost

You're poor and father's dad and never come
down from Boston to the city to meet me
    so I never see your face
and miss you, Morris, my friend. I'm not only
sentimental but feel your anonymity
    as my own lost bag.

Is your black maid, Harriet, a legal wife?
Where are the children? Bits of gossip
    about the widower.
You must be the short tailor out of Poland.
I've been to Krakow and seen Copernicus's
    glass eye that held the night,

and like his planets you revolve around
the sun. Close to Krakow is Auschwitz where
    I looked at baby shoes,
and poor suits you would have cut
had you not taken a steamer in 1887
    to Boston, still eating herring

and speaking your Jewish German. Mean?
I'm caught between you and father.
    You live a few seconds
in a Sunday morning phone call.
You hit on Dad for a hundred bucks. He shouts,
    'The only thing you ever gave me

was your belt.' Let anger and boring
chronicles end. I'm not lying, I care for you
    and glad you're not a poet
with a pocket stuffed with words. You make vests
and coats and we talk about the art of cutting
    cloth. You squeeze my hand

and invent me. A Sancho Panza
of the sniping word, you scissor me this evening.
    I'm your age. Your voice sticks in
as a sewing needle pricking my finger,
making sure I'll stay around. I'm here.
    We know the loneliness of work.

You say, 'I cut, you write. Some are dogs,
some birds.' And I say, 'You are a cloth ghost
    I'm looking for in a grave.'
'No, Billy, you've come. You're my grandson.
We've wasted lots of time, but we can keep
    meeting in some old book.'

Giving a Watch Life

'The body is an animated machine.'

René Descartes

Repair me, watchmaker. Insert your tool
into my chest, its oscillating spring,
my heart, and screw the spindle in the jewel
and the frail balance wheel of steel will ring
in silence while its tense mainspring will store
my spunk to last a day. Then close the case
and I'll hop downtown to a lover. Poor
in discipline and peace, now in my race
with night, I'll own another day to tick
and tick. But fix me just a bit. I want

my sweet to feel my movement, touch the dial,
to open me and poke around. Then sick
of perfect gears, she'll blow on dust and haunt
my parts and kiss me out of time a while.

Wings of the Morning

If I take the wings of the morning
and dwell in the uttermost parts of the sea
or knee my way up from cloud to cloud and find the mist
      won't hold me,
or plunge into hell and make my bed of poisons there,
you are also there,
my echo, and I your echo, you who frame me with the echo
      of the first morning of being,
who knit me out of the earth which in secret you mix
      with my blood.

If I take the wings of the morning and fly toward your hand,
you receive me a monster and child in the pit of dream
where I ponder implacable extinction with no escape into light,
and though you are nameless we shadows converse
and go to villages, wake early on a secret meadow
where we climb to a morning mountain of secluded high grass,

And when every joint screams, when I stumble alone
in the dim prison of me with no old key from Toledo
      to give false hope,
when there is no one, none, when zero is my frame, even then
      in extreme silence
I take the wings of the morning and hang onto impossible winds,
and wherever I drift you are with me.

Thou Among the Wastes

Time is a ferryboat lumbering one way
for each of us, yet floating endlessly,
porting new customers for a quick lay.
Shakespeare in sonnets cursed the husbandry
of hideous time which, cultivating death,
defaces us. Yet ferries hold their course,
ferrying you, allowing me a breath
of life, until we drown below the floors
of rock where no time shines. I wonder how
I've lasted while the young collapse. William
himself died young but not before he got
his feather pen to decorate a bough
with wrinkled suns against the cold. I am
his ship of wormy time, blessing his rot.

from
The Secret Reader

The Secret Reader

I write my unread book for you who in
a life or day will find it in a box
or cave or dead man's pocket or the inn
of mountain light where we awake while cocks
of twilight scream our solitude. Our fate
is to be free. No public ink. No hot
or cold inferno of the private wait.
Just this apocryphon which I forgot
for you, the secret friend. You are like me:
one soul fleshed out for ecstasy and night,
this planet's only birth and death, unknown
like all. The gospels falsified the light,
for no one rose again. We are alone,
alive with secret words. Then blackly free.

Gas Lamp, 1893

In brownstone Boston down on old Milk Street,
up two gray flights, near the gas lamp, the tailor
waits glumly for the midwife. August heat
has worn the woman out. Amid the squalor
she looks around the bed, clutching a cape
she brought from London as a child. It's dawn
and dirty. The dark tailor wants to escape
to his cramped shop. The woman's sheets are drawn
below her waist. She isn't hollering now.
Her eyes are dark and still; blood on her thumbs.
Her name is Bessie. No. I'm guessing. How,
untold, am I to know? Hot day has worn
into the room. The midwife finally comes.
Grandmother bleeds to death. My father's born.

Grandfather

Born over there, in mist, not even God
or Germans have a record of the house
or village outside Vilna. Here, the old
poor tyrant snips a cloth, stitches a blouse
or shirt, and finds a black woman to live
with when his wife is dead. His smart son sells
papers in Boston subways, won't forgive
the tyrant fool for whipping him. The smells
of steam and cooking mix with yellow cheeses
when suddenly the wrathful tailor seizes
a belt and flogs his son for rotten grades!
Last drama. Twelve years old, my father leaves
his home and school for good. The tailor fades
from all of us forever, stitching clothes.

Bowdoin, 1948

Hawthorne once had this yellowed room. We share
the morning gloom of alcoholics or
nocturnal masturbators, north and nowhere,
too isolated for a date or whore.
Were you a grind like me? A dreamer slob
and weird? I sleep, the window open to
the black Maine snow, hearing my roommate throb
and scream, an epileptic getting through
another siege. He's a philosopher;
I'm lost. But he was born a bastard, he
says bitterly; my origins I shirk
from. Worst (or best?) I doubt there is a me
concocting words in terrifying blur
within. Dream, Hawthorne. Words no longer work.

Rocking on the Queen

Deep in the hold we have no porthole, yet
I gaze, X-raying whales and a green squall.
The pitching of ELIZABETH has set
the tables rolling, banging wall to wall.
I push up to the deck and wait for France.
At twenty I'm a character whom Plato
might keep for lunch, yet the Greek's reasoned trance
is not my Bergson dream. I'm a potato
head says my Marxist pal. Norm's blind but grins
at me. Naive! As Europe nears, wet shade
washes my eyes with reverie. I dry
my face. Europe is full of women. Inns
of smart delicious lips. We dock. The maid
at l'Hotel Flore pinches my pants and tie.

In a Paris Faubourg

My Polish classmate at the gray Sorbonne
loves the romantic poet Bécquer. She
wears heavy wool, is Chopin-thin and fun
in Paris rain. One night she secrets me
off to a grim Free Polish Army party
up in an orange room. We're comrades and
march behind banners down Boule Miche. Hearty
and generous in she takes my hand
a Sunday morning; we go to a faubourg,
a sleazy house. I don't guess why. 'It's clear',
she says. 'I'm pregnant and abortion's not
a legal act in France.' Up in the morgue
the foreign doctor cuts her up. 'So, here
is your chef-d'oeuvre', he tells me. We are rot.

White Island

My first day at the school for Constantine
I meet a peasant father with two hooks
(wounds from Albania) and the German Queen
of Greece who loans me her blue *Faber Book
of Verse*. But soon I'm fired and so begin
to loaf and write on islands. Mykonos,
the iceberg. I'm the only *xenos* in
the village, living with a Greek, and close
to getting jailed for working without papers.
The ship comes twice a week. Down at the pier
we all watch who comes in, but lemon vapors
of broiling fish seduce me. One white night
Captain Andonis slaps his heels. Austere,
he teaches me to dance, to live on light.

One Andalusian Winter

It's early Franco Spain. Hunger of serfs
and fishermen like insects sleeping on
the sand under their boats. When morning surfs
into the village we pick up fresh prawn
and goat meat. Justo's all upset. They caught
and killed some *rojos* in the hills, and threw
the bodies over horses which they've brought
into the plaza on their way up to
the old Phoenician common grave of Jews.
Our farm—with sugar cane and orange trees,
with snow magnolias—is a paradise
almost for nothing. Lorca's a man of vice,
un loco to his fascist cousin who's
our mayor. Laughing I grieve by these old seas.

Boot Camp in Georgia

'Yeah', shouts the corporal, 'all Jewmen fall out!'
A black kid and me, we go to pick up
our 3 day pass from Dix. 'What's it about?'
'Jewish New Year.' They fly us with our pup
tent, boots and duffle down to Georgia where
still on the airstrip a white sergeant blurts,
'Sound out your name and race!' We're in the fair
sweet South. 'I'll squeeze that bastard till he squirts
white piss', the black kid whispers. I get stuck
three days on K.P. God what grease! I feel
good here. No anti-intellectual crap
of campuses. I catch pneumonia but heal
fast and they treat me good. Have friends and rap.
I don't have to kill. It's peace. What the fuck!

Yale

Sterling Library is a confession booth
where Virgil hangs out on a shelf by stars
gold on the ceiling calm and beaming truth
and blueblood aristocracy. Guitars
are out. I haunt the books, reading Jack Donne
who kisses metaphysically. In class
I'm shy and tongue tied among gentlemen
and lovely women scholars. What a gas
to eat at Louie's, peddle to East Haven,
play with my infant daughter now become
my lifelong sun. With stupid discipline
I race through (gone for good the wandering bum
of Europe) yet among my peers I'm craven:
no pilgrimage to Ezra in his loony bin.

Secret Meadow in Vermont

Vermont was made by Andrew Marvell when
his solitude was green with mountain night.
Yellow meadow lying under the pen
of twilight sun. Rays scrawl on weeds with white
of the astonished moon. Three stars persist
while crickets rattle on the phone of wind
to bugs. Birds call up worms. Deer feel the fist
of grass about them. Our goat Smoky grinned
at us last afternoon when he took off.
He's back this morning, trampling on a rug
of black eyed Susans. Drunk, minus signs on
his eyes, he leads us with his mocking cough
up to the secret meadow. Marvell, gone
into green shade, is laughing in his mug.

Near Annapurna

We are still at cloud level. Beautiful day.
Thin air. Cold but our sweat warms us. The snow
jungle of rhododendrons weirdly gray
around the deadly trail. My friend starts to blow
up, bitching, 'Don't come too close!' A mule went
over the ledge an hour ago. We inch
down a stone cliff. ANNAPURNA. Indifferent
white continent. I can't make it. I clinch
the ice, crawl the ravine. As snow turns to mud
I slide on my buns. It's raining. Beautiful
hot rain almost washes us off the top.
We find a smoky cabin. I'm full of blood.
Go in feverishly filthy, dirty wool,
drink a pot of hot lemon juice, and flop.

The Camp near Kraków

Over the gate the sign ARBEIT MACHT FREI.
I guess my village outside Vilna, which
was razed, came here in cattle cars to die.
Today it's raining on the Kraków church,
its peaceful domes, and on the camp which is
a gray museum. I see the children's skulls,
the shaven heads of Jews and gypsies, Poles,
photos of eyes like prehistoric flies
stuck on the walls outside the shower room
in which the rain prepared the bodies for
the ovens and the sky where bodies bloom.
ARBEIT MACHT FREI. Auschwitz is mute, the war
already fugitive. The rains evoke
a Slav, black hatted Jews, tattoos and smoke.

The Spring Afternoon Aliki in Her Third Year
Starts to Drown

No melancholy yet. You are a green
planet on which a darkness only lives
to obscure death. But no one sees you lean
over the pond. We all are fugitives
from our New Haven, at a festival
of arts in the woods. For fun you toss a stone
onto the water. Suddenly, you fall
in it, unseen! Your gold hair sails alone
at the far end where you were playing. You
float, limbs spread like a leaf. One minute more
and you will be extinct. A painter spots
the passive form, dives toward it. I jump too.
We drag you out, pump air through you before
you enter myth, before your beauty rots.

With My Redneck Sons in Southern Indiana

The pampas of America begin
north of our barn. Glaciers smoothed down the earth
for buffalo and corn, but I live in
the poor south hills where farmland isn't worth
the taxes, and the KKK comes out
of the wet Gothic woods. Our humpbacked barn
is rusty in the patient twilight. Scout-
ing the Blue River bendable as yarn
or glowworms, I am not quite Baptist red-
neck like my sons who often paddle through
the bluffs. But in a barn I placed a bed
and desk and dreamt the world. Gone from the coast,
I camp on hills of vanished Indians a few
calm nights and hear trees talk. I'm still a ghost.

Billy Budd

Billy knew how to make the ocean ring
with cloud-birds or the humming monsters in
the deep. The Handsome Sailor, mimicking
the illiterate nightingale, climbed up to win
his supper from the stars, and sang. He sang
tunes he made up to larger seafowl scream-
ing near the foretop. Barely a child of time,
from the maintop the angel had to hang,
for gagged by lies he had no words when quick
as flame from a night cannon his right arm
shot out and Claggart dropped. So through the mist
Billy ascended, and ascending took
the full rose of the dawn. Wordless his charm,
sleepy, now oozy weeds about him twist.

With a French Nun in Lapland

Even the constant sun wears a small coat
of darkness till it bangs into our light.
A nun in Lapland on a ferry boat,
whose lips are frozen God, whose hood is white
with ice floating the fjords, unzips my pants
to show her grace. 'I'll keep this memory',
she whispers, 'in my bones and sardine cans
back in the factory where I share my tea
and labor with the workers.' Sun hangs on
all night in Lapland in July. I bless
my friend the nun for sun. A socialist
and French she talked to clouds over our fun
and deer licks. When our bellies join, no less
than mountains blush and crush us in their fist.

Lapland

The roots of the earth protrude
down into the pinegray ocean
and up into the glacial snow.

There are not many fir trees
as we push into the unreal
north. We are beyond the green

and on nude scrubby earth again.
Here where snow yawns into the
sea, and air is clean like fish,

distance and form and seasons
are more true than the odd boat
or village. Time. This land is

dream; planet where almost no one
is; or if real, then quick cities
south are dream before the slow

iceland. At night sunshine floats
on big mountain ribs of snow;
gulls cry and cod run in the ocean.

Song of the Birds

After Pablo Casals had taped the Song
of the Birds, high on Canigo, we went
by foot, from the old French convent, along
the mountain rug of stars, down to the scent
of wheat. We couldn't see. You held my hand
because the trail was steep. Then in the grove
we saw ourselves. Naked. By the command
of natural soul, we lay down young and drove
our blood. Our tongues were water, our eyes huge,
earth an unknowing fire until the dawn
of cows and village children screaming led
us back. I loved you in our pure refuge
against the law. The night was sun. Though gone,
our virgin mountain is a lucent thread.

Rapping with God in the Kitchen

God blows into the kitchen. I'm undressed.
I've just dashed back from trying to sneak outside,
naked, to throw you off. 'We will arrest
you for lascivious carriage', you tell me snide-
ly. I compose myself. 'God, be my friend.
Don't haunt or dream me. I'm no punching bag
and yet your fingers whisper I must end
this whim of peace without you. Let's relax,
sit down, slug a few beers and chew the rag.
Maybe in nightmare you will drop your mask,
reveal your eyes, be gentle and be known.
You're all I have,' I say in weakness, 'but
for God's sake, show your face.' At this, you cut
me off and fade. My lies work best alone.

The Whisper

Sometimes I'm happy. Then the yellow cry
of sun roams in my ear, especially
if I'm in a dark room alone. I see
loud light! I float. Sometimes I want to die
and dream that Plato will instruct my soul
with secrets of our being before that leap
when I have slammed the final door of sleep.
I'm neither beaming nor about to roll
over and croak. I am resigned. I'm not
nature or you, but just one mind confined
to ink, and even this typed page is signed
like a fake portrait. Now, my clumsy thought
uses your alien words as if I could
howl my whisper beyond this fading wood.

A Rose in Hell

After slopping through hell along three roads,
I stumble on a rose. Insane? A flower
in this dark land where we hop dark like toads
in darkness. Beasts. I hear Moscow's red hour
of revolt. No. I am too tired, too old
not to reform. Too much bathos of hell.
My tape plays old French songs. White rose. A bell
wakes the grand organ of the Czar. I've sold
my house, bought an exhilaration shoe
to walk beyond the Caucasus. I try,
goodbye. I'm really well, and will fall on
a resurrection. Don't tell me I lie.
Can I get out? I'm almost tunneling through
to ice, a secret rose, and blizzard dawn.

Spirit Has a Beginning

Although there's no Director of the Scenes
working especially for me, I bet
what happens is for good. Forgot my jeans
in Hong Kong; on a marble hill in Crete
I left a lens. Yesterday in Nepal
a boy got my glasses. Why do I lose
my things? Alms to the cosmos? When I fall
in love, it lasts a life, but I confuse
my lover, lose her, and walk for years
on fire. It's good. Rain will surprise my heart
one day before I die. Theologies
despise possessions, and I feel no tears
for things—though lost love replays death. Yet these
words come because I lose. Loss is a start.

Genesis

In the beginning God made heaven and
the earth, which were invisible, unformed,
with darkness over the abyss. God warmed
the waters with his breath. Then his command:
'Let there be light.' And there was light. He saw
the light, that it was beautiful. God's ray
entered the mire of light and through the draw
of darkness, and he called the morning day.
Then God said, 'Let there be a firmament
amid the waters, let it grow between
water and water.' In such way God made
and named a sky, splitting the waters laid
on earth from rains above. That boundless tent
became our heaven and its air was green.

Apollo in Náxos

Huge kouros on its back and not alive,
not even finished, but the eyes are blur
of mountains behind mountains under five
layers of mist; the huge lips are a slur
of rocky lust, never to kiss or talk.
Life as stone is simple: the mammoth arm
intense yet calm in the gold marble lock
of time. I'm never still and seldom calm
and feel a fly's six twitching legs. The dark
profiles of mountains of the night are never
enough to burn a way of gold, a spark
of cosmic life. The soul is soul, stone stone.
The kouros stares into the air forever,
a phantom of live rock. We're each alone.

Gospel of Lies

Comrade illusion, I embrace you like
a tuba. Gold and false. My hero Don
Quijote rose up mad and set his pike
against the gales of mills and monsters on
the wasteland of La Mancha. Jesus al-
so toured, performing magic, and he gave
his life so we might drink the alcohol
of heaven, drink the light and be no slave
of truth. Even the Buddha found a way
to free the unsubstantial self and fly
inside a dream of sun. Until the sun
was gone Quijano lived the noble lie
of lunacy: the poor man with a day
of grace and fire. Then true oblivion.

W.B. Was Born and Died

The rolling dice came up with Willis. Am
I me? Even my death is nothing more
than confirmation of an epigram:
W.B. WAS BORN AND DIED. The roar
of being is all I know. I hear it, yes,
and neither I nor you can think beyond
this oddity, this arbitrariness
that makes us locked like Earth—a vagabond
of planets in a thinning glove of air—
locked in a universe of mindless things.
The moon has no idea it has no soul.
And yet this heart, this ticking being, a hair
that holds it live, these wheels of love, these strings
of hope, I'd know, though soon I will be coal.

Franz Kafka in His Small Room on the Street of the Alchemists, 1916–1917

One winter Kafka rented a white room
high near the castle where he tired his pen
during the day. At night he rinsed the gloom
out of his eyes and was a crow in heaven,
rising, dancing on awful heights. Before
dawn fed him sleep, the Golem far below
the wall whispered a grave song in his ear
in ancient Hebrew vague to him. Although
he slept, the ghost of Jewish friends in Prague
(Max Brod who loved his ink) helped him
survive close to the sky. A winter wood
of horses floated on the city fog.
The castle mastered him, but in a whim
he drank white ink and hungered where he stood.

Gospel of the Magadalena in the Garden

As Mary turned to leave the tomb, she heard,
'Woman, why are you weeping?' It must be
the gardener, she thought. 'Because my lord
is gone', she said. 'They've taken him away.
I came with spices for his body.' When
she looked again two angels robed in white
were in the empty tomb. Then on that night
of loss and vision in Jerusalem,
of death made miracle, the Magdalene
went through the alleys to her mat, lay down,
and in an evening blue as paradise
she knew the gardener was God. So John
told us. What hope without her stratagem
of faith? She dreamt beyond the funeral spice.

Mary's Version

The Christians stole my life. I was a Jew,
an unembellished wife and mother till
the Romans pounded nails in Josh. It's true
he coughed up magic parables, but kill
a guy for that? Then Matt, Mark, Luke and John
gossiped with visionaries, dreamt up tales,
made me unreal and cast him as a con-
man, yes, a stuntman popping miracles
to fool the world. Their curve on history
was holy gospel lies and my despair.
The facts: I never went to rallies in
the fields, Josh wasn't God, I had my spin
with Joe, and Joshua was our son. I swear
there is no bastard in my family tree.

Tree of Life

Beijing, 1984

Don't cry for me. The Tree of Life
is full of birds. When I was old
in winter, lonely as a knife,
and when my heart was blue and cold,
I fell in love. Don't cry for me.
The Tree of Life is lilac
and smells of May and poverty,
poor as an orchard of bamboo.
I fell in love when I was young
and now I'm crazy once again,
in jail with jasmine on my tongue
and in my heart a cyclamen.
Don't cry for me. I'm young again
and every spring is cyclamen.

A Fly

Wesleyan, 1956

On this hot day of shame my body walks
in sweaty clothes with cuffs rolled at the elbow,
dreaming beyond the view where my eye balks—
a fly, trapped, craving space beyond the window.
Apathy. Habitude. Even the weather
puts the fire out. And daily this and that
calms my hill horse, confining it in leather,
and tames the moon, the nightly acrobat.
This humid weather seethes inside my flesh.
I see no dome of light, no diamond beach,
no holy God to halt the minute gun,
yet like the fly buzzing against the mesh
my body feels the sky it cannot reach
and craves the darkness of the alien sun.

The Lilies

The lilies in the field below a sphere
of half moons in the rain, of fowls and moths,
go unclothed, do not spin or toil or hear
the prayer of Solomon in radiant cloths
and yet their nakedness is perfect snow
under whose milky galaxies the seed
lies comatose. The lilies only grow
and burn. Their meditation is to feed
on light. Naked of thought, a multitude
by the day Adam learned to stand, these plants
are human, living in chance villages
like breezy monks sworn to dumb elegance.
When thrown into the oven, no lord says
a word. The lilies fall in solitude.

The Nightingale

Although the horror of the nightingale,
the holy nightingale who sings unheard,
invisible and strident in the gale
beyond the tree of stars, is just a word
or region of epistemology,
I wake to it like breakfast when my eye
of pus is washed to meet the ecstasy
of day. Horror is never far: the dry
biology of insect hope, the moth
trapping the moon, the wasp of solitude
amid the panting of the air, the cloth
of flying worms. And yet I always hear
the secret of the nightingale, delud-
ing me. Invisibly I'm almost here.

from
African Bestiary

The Giraffe Is the Grand Philosopher of Africa

Twiga

The giraffe stands in huge gentility,
   A solitary tower
On the savanna. Next to his family,
   Brooding with silent power,
He guards the oaken-color plain against
   The springing carnivore
Who wants his sleeping young for lunch. A fence
   Of stone, this herbivore

Will not retreat. His eyes are cruel. No sack
   Of Disney gush, he glares
With globes of hate. If predators attack,
   With blacksmith hoofs he tears
Their feline eyes out, cracks their ribs. Don't mess
   With the tall male giraffe.
For lion or lusty leopard who gives chase
   He wields his legs as staffs

To smash the enemy. When safe, he goes
   To a far hill where his troop
Of leaning towers treads the evening blue
   Savanna. Now in the loop
Of war and peace, this giant stands in peace.
   Keen in the twilight breeze,
A silent sly Diogenes from Greece,
   Brooding in floating ease,

Our giraffe is the grand philosopher
   Of Africa, a Plato
Inscribed with spots of light near snouts of fear.
   No underground potato,
The giraffe looms outdoors—never in caves—
   Where he's both sentinel
And sky dweller. His cloud-high eyeballs save
   His young from feline hell.

The spy giraffe notes everything that is.
   Believe in her. She's wise
Like the grand elephant. Their threatened bliss
   Survives in mammoth thighs.
Now, a giraffe leans low, sprints from the herd
   And gulps three stars of grass.
On the far hill see grace of the huge bird
   Of floating steel and glass.

Lion Sleeps with One Eye Open

Simba

The lion sleeps with one eye open to the dawn.
His third eye dreams HE is the militant of God,
Who after disappearing for three days will yawn
Back into life and save us from the mortal sod.
Yet normally the monarch lion wakes by sun
And with a mortal bite he chokes a zebra for
His pride of golden ladies and his cubs, and one
Day when the sun strolls on a cloud, with a mad roar
He leaps into the sky, and with a mammoth bite
Swallows the sunstar, blackening the earth in night.
Now, lions are the handsomest of quadrupeds,
But watch out for these feline charmers in their pride,
Who with a scream will turn a world to dread!
Tame killers, if you can, or keep them on your side.

Leopard Dancer

Chui

The leopard is a Rudolph Valentino
Tangoing in trees. Manzanilla Fina
Can't match the fine dry elegance that floats
About his limbs and limber leopard coat.
Prince of the predators, he springs from no-
Where down. Even the half-ton buffalo
Has no escape. The big cat tears the left haunch
Right off the bull, hauls it up to his branch
And chews it for a week. This warrior likes
His bloody supper after his quick spikes
Of death have won him game. The dancer lies
Out in the sun, enjoying his meat pies.

Rhinoceros Is a Beauty

Faru

The rhino is superb, a beauteous thing
    Among all animals.
In Nepal he's majestic like their king,
    The tyrant hunter all

In knightly armor, who each year shot one tiger.
    In Africa he's plain,
Solitary, black or white. He too is farmer
    In his own terrain,

Renewing earth while munching grass. He'll charge
    If you usurp his space.
I have stood quiet by him, by his large
    Abundantly strange face.

Love him, his horn for which the Chinese kill
    For aphrodisiacs.
The rhino is superb, a beauteous thing,
    A loner animal

Standing beside a river or a spring,
    His meditation hall.
His only threat—extermination. Chill
    Out. Beauty won't attack.

His horn, a cutlass in bold ivory,
    Can make you climb a tree
In fear. But fear no rhino. Fear the clap
    And tyrants, not this chap.

Hippopotomus Racing at Night

Kiboko

By day the hippo is submerged on river sand.
By night the tubby beast roams up to graze the land.

Stumpy legs and huge bulk, he's safe from predators
Except for man who wants his blubber and abhors

Him trampling crops. In sun or lake he basks a while
Though may attack small boats, thinking them crocodiles.

He seems to be a Disney prop, a bloated bull,
Tranquil, funny, benign, never caring to brawl.

Untrue. He's fast as shit on wheels, ready to kill,
And if you block his way you better take a pill

Since you're about to die! Sometimes he's near your house,
Foraging your lawn. Neither villain nor a mouse,

The hippo will protect its calf, its path and food.
Gaze at this wonder. Keep him in a gentle mood.

Warthog Is the Imaginary Beast

Gwasi, Mbango or Ngiri

Even your name is ugly, as if eyes of mud
And excrement had fashioned you as blood
Of the grotesque. How wrong! Good hog with ties
To common pigs, when gods made you, their eyes
Were blindfolded. Yet you, hairy brown busts
Of faux sublime, ferocious with your tusks,
Two pairs out of your mouth spook all wild cats
Of prey. Your trot is slow across the flats.

One look at you, you're safe. No looking glass
Will call you cute like rabbits in the grass.
The enemy of grace, you invent sports
Of bachelor sex with four forbidding warts,
Defenses on your head against the thrusts
Of other males in mating fights. Your lusts
Are big, your housing poor. You dig into
Abandoned aardvark burrows. What you do

Is enter ass-end first and then burst out
Into the night, smashing foes with your snout.
All things considered, *Señor Oddity*,
In heaven you'll find sleep; on earth fungi
Roots, berries, eggs, and even a dead bird.
Your sight is poor, rich your survival word.
By day you scan to be no cheetah's feast.
By night you are the imaginary beast.

Ibis in Egypt Is Thoth

Korongo domo-njano

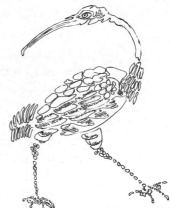

In Egypt he is Thoth, an ibis head
    On a standing man's body
Or the full bird is god-judge of the dead,
    Inventor of astronomy,

Magic, writing, and even the first word.
    No bird or beast can boast
Such aristocracy of thought as this bird
    Ibis wading on the coast

      These days (no longer painted on tomb blocks),
        And her nobility
      Compares in diamonds to the awkward walk
        Of storks beside the sea.

      Here both compete for fish and surf insects.
        That ibis-headed man
      As bird is sacred still. She counts stars, detects
        Each shadow on the sand

      For precious food, and as a force for thought,
        She stands in meditation
      Of what she was and is and how she ought
        To be in each mutation.

Spider a Weaver with Eight Eyes

Buibui

Like Annie Albers at her loom,
The spider is the technocrat
Among the artists. In her room
Her weave is fine and never fat.

Assuming every whim of space,
Breaking Da Vinci's secret frown,
Only a mirror knows her ways
Of spinning silk while upside down.

She plots a kill with her eight eyes
And eight quick legs. Then spots the fly.
As engineer of ancient fear,

While dreaming guts and a cold beer,
She lets him twist in her fine mesh.
Then dives and dines on his sweet flesh!

Oryx

Choraoa

The bush is bare, a lot of low
Thorn-tree acacias and the brush.
Beasts aren't fussy where they go:
Oryx the beautiful in lush

Savanna, arid bush or shine
Of desert where her tracks are seen
From helicopters as a sign
Of visitors from outer green

Planets. They step on earth with grace,
Know when to fight and when to flee,
Well trained by maestros back in space,
Though here they're hunted ruthlessly.

They race as four types of *Gazelle*
Oryx, all with long sloping horns,
Whose thrust sends lions into hell,
Whose profile gave the unicorn

To smart mythologists. New calves
Run with the herd right after birth.
Faces painted with crisscross staves,
Their giraffe legs sparkle the earth.

Oryx are beautiful and tough,
Their gemsbok horns are scimitars.
In bush or desert when it's gruff
And dry, they survive without water.

Don't hunt the sacred oryx, gem
Of Araby. When shot, great shame.
The Hebrew Bible calls her *re'em*
Writ unicorn in the King James.

The White Unicorn in China, India, Africa, and Le Musée de Cluny in Paris

Qilin

Many have written of the unicorn
from Pliny to Rilke. Then back to wise
Confucius immeasurably forlorn
on hearing that the unicorn is slain. His eyes

mourn the fallen beast. Emperor Genghis Khan
about to invade India meets a horse
with deer body and one white horn, who bans
this new calamity: 'Forgo your bloody course.'

The imaginary beast of continents
duels with harsh warlords with his horn of peace.
Like moody gods and poetry he sometimes vents

anger and noise, but then soars high like geese.
Psalm 22 sings, 'Save us from the time
of unicorns', but on the African savannah
the oryx profile spellbinds like Nirvana.

Now the beast wanders like a hungry rhyme.
A Paris virgin takes him to her lap.
In amazed tapestry her love becomes his trap.

Peacock

Dausi

The peacock is the Sun King of the birds,
Louis Quatorze but in captivity
With no poor workers leaping to his words.
His feathered splendor glows for fans to see.

He is the pet of beauty on a farm,
Not in the bush for hunters or wild teeth.
His arrogance is slow and does no harm
To subjects since he has none. He's a wreath

Of poetry to amuse a wishful Yeats
Deep in the Congo, formed by nature's eye
Green like his train, but when he lifts his tail

To mate he grows enormous like a whale.
This pheasant, no way peasant, struts and eats
Until his owner pines for peacock pie!

Cuckoo Whose Note Makes Me Float

Mtombo

The Cuckoo is a bird   whose bell is heard
When her name is said.   Then a bell of lead
Becomes a sphere   of silver to the ear
And every tree   blooms like a dappled sea
Of fruit and mist,   and every hill is kissed
With *cuckoo cuckoo   echo echo* too
Beautiful for song.   the cuckoo is not for long
In his love nest,   but lays his eggs to rest
Each night with a   new love, then flits away.
I am surprised and pleased   to hear her seized
With tricks, content   on the first continent
With her own flock   of thorn trees. Soon I'll dock
Far from her thorn   trees here. I'm nor forlorn.
As stars appear,   never can she disappear
Or cease her cuckoo note   making me float.

Baboon an Expert in Frivolity

Nyani
Papio cynocephalus

If you're called *baboon*, you're a moron,
The name was made up by Comte de Buffon,
And even in Latin *cynocephalus*,
'Doghead' is not an admirable plus.

Baboons are experts in frivolity.
Riding bareback on her mom, a baby
Standing on a furry back hops slaphappy
To a first cousin in the family.

The family is key. Like the raccoon
Bandit baboons are acrobats and lun-
atics. They're everywhere. Gangs steal the seed
Of newly planted fields, a troop to weed

Each fated grain of wheat as it were grass,
And soon the meadow's bare as their pale ass.
Their hairless comfort pad of flesh is typical
Of these forever jumpy animals

Who look for ways to creep into some cheap
Blimps filled with food and float off like balloons,
But all have conked out dreaming into sleep
Like wildflowers snoring under prairie moons.

Owl

Babewana

The owl is a hoot. The poet Edgar Allan Poe
　　Hears her nocturnal howl,
And gothic and ubiquitous he lets her crow
　　Bell through his verse. The owl

Is far-sighted and turns her telescopic eye
　　A hundred eighty degrees
So she can see her prey. She is the perfect spy.
　　In Zanzibar her species

Likes the rain forest. It is dense unlike the plain.
　　In sunlight almost blind,
At night she turns her head and spots you daylight plain
　　And soon her beak or claw

Will crash into your neck. In Greece when I was young
　　I heard the nightingale
And owl, a garden duet vying for their song
　　To reach a lover. I

Prefer to let this evening predator be heard
　　So the young squirts will sigh
And old farts recall, and not make her sin as absurd
　　Bigoted beast-tales do,

Calling up her Semitic nose and treachery. She's wise
　　And is Athena's friend
Companion. In this malarial forest she cries.
　　To an unseen star she lends

Her passion, making its remote inhabitants
　　Connect with us. That's more
Than even dreaming Poe could dream, whose bleak tales dance
　　To the owl's nocturnal roar.

Dove

Fumvu

The dove is peace. Slam her as raven, crow,
Pigeon or any tribal slur, the dove
Is peace. She is a dream, and dreamers know,
As Bill Blake sees and Dante can't, that love
Is truth, not terza rima sky, nor curse
Of Christian punishment, nor grace. Blake bows
To chimney sweepers. black boy, a whore's hearse;
And visionary Blake is peace and now,

His heart bigger than don Quijote's nag.
Noah sends out a dove over the flood
To see where land begins. Hope is her tag.
After Jesus is circumcised, his blood
Is on his parent's hand. They sacrifice
Two doves to bring their son good luck.
John of the Cross implores a dove's advise
And flies high like a dove, drops into muck

To find mystical love. His dove is white
And finds her in the dark night of the soul.
A laughing dove eats fruit and seeds to fight
Off hunger. Saints and doves cry from a hole.
Will peace calm plains of lion and the lamb?
Will murder cease on Kenya's wild savanna?
Will poacher dine with ranger, and build a dam,
Fill common waterholes for dove and raptor?

from
Antijournal
&
A Snow Salmon Reached
The Andes Lake

God

They made me.
Gave me a white hippy beard
And my throat sang
A loud cuckoo and the godly nightingale
And they heard.

I was a star
In the morning of their book,
A fly at noon,
A beast in their chest, angel in their ribs,
A purple hat.

I was king,
Sun, frog, a lily that lived
In the winter.
They wouldn't let me die amid the murder
From the clocks.

I was a bell,
A cowbell and clavier. At dawn
My whole light
Woke the bubble of the earth, burned its edge,
Blew me inside!

They made me
And unmade me. My best friends
Left. I hang
Around the old neighborhood, lonely man
Behind the times.

My good friends
Suffer for truth. I was their face,
Their joyful lie.
They need me. I make their day ridiculous
And cast them

Alone in the dark.
I was a morning star. Now
I'm nothing. Zero.
They've got nothing like me. Before I left
I made light.

Chapel

Midnight and observation jeeps parked by the Acheron
and the unexplored temple
and prison at Oropos with the composer.
We hear fever in our lungs
and climb carefully on blue mountains
on the blue ledge over the bay of Euboia
to Saint Peter's small chapel
where we talk and love all night,
a night of milk
and fresh oranges you bring when we are tired.
Our white bird is no dream as it rains
through the tender dark.
The secret police are sleeping in the room
beside the royalist officers who failed.
Ferry boats begin to cross the grape morning bay.
At dawn you ask my name.

```
    U L
 F     L
 M     N
 O O
```

As a white dome in a romantic eye
    I've had my day
        Soon
    They will know me,
Explore each contour of my dusty body.

My people no longer bring figs and milk
    When they lie down
        Deep
    In mountain grass.
Only a few still glare at my white thigh.

But I am good. Honeycomb. Meadow of light,
    And you can feed
        On
    My massive shape,
Which can plunge into your eye! I am still

A woman to floor you. An electric bulb,
    I can turn off,
        On,
    Or dance my beam,
The one huge female belly drinking you.

Dream

Maybe these poems (which are half my life)
and my life too are not worth more
than guano or Pedro Domeq or a few drachma
        on a ton of phosphate. If so,
I would be pleased to leave now
for I am no son of the Buddha
or even of Jesus who came from my dark blood.
I am more a lobster in its pound.
Yes, I stay a child with a cunning dream of waking up,
unafraid of time, released, an orphan free.

Cello

Tonight I take cross and a coke bottle
        and heave them in the sea
and have to dance very late alone in my room
where the two oil lamps laugh dryly,
Maybe I am learning how to act.

Your face is luminous and happy when you
     surprise me at the door;
you sit on your nightgown and we embrace.
All night the cello plays outside and wanders
        on the red rooftops in the Sporades.
By dawn we are so fragile. We are alone and dance;
then dress slowly by the fire of the owls.
Outside the crane's wing shines in the rose
        of the early sun.
Your face is gone and glows.

Morning of Herbs

I take your hand. In it are the fields
of thyme and the camomile apple groves we pick.
How many mornings of herbs are there?
Enough for two lives? After midnight we drive in falling snow.
Streets grow soft. Snow hides the Christmas fire
and the paper farmhouse in us that is to burn.
From the seaport we follow an orange butterfly into a warm apple
grove.
I put a cardboard bird in your arms.
It is our last day
and so we briefly die on the fragrant meadow.

Wild Iris

In the small scholarly room
where we live freely between books and lions
on a mountain of light,
the window over our bed cannot shut
and a winter moon freezes on us.
We lie close and keep warm under a Finnish drape
When you get up to pee or wash
your soft return is a fawn in the iris
of a wild brook.
We are distinguished and perfect.

When you type and type through the dawn
and I the scholar of one candle
write and doze,
we meander freely like the goats in the sun
in the broken marble reading rooms
of Asian Pergamon.
Our room is frozen. You type. I hug you,
make you tea and we keep warm.

Lions of Delos

Even in crazy gloom in the center of fools I lie
    and daydream
of being that huge torso of Apollo lying cracked
    and serene on the beach
near the palm tree near the gold bridge
    from the ship called Parabola.

I lie. I see us
hand in hand along the sea urchin shore
    near the plaza of heat and fig trees.
We walk from the torso to the row of canine lions,
    archaic stone pitted with sun,
gazing alive like us at the Aegean Sea way out.

Way out.
It is a yellow boat. It comes and now is lost in haze
Beyond the Theologian's cave and summit of monks;
beyond the high chalk village and nothing.
Revelation in the haze.
Though our common cloud of unknowing
    we love and grope
toward a bit of snow we cannot see.

The Island of Patmos

The dream ends here. Beyond these solitary whales
    and seven stars
we wake. Here is peace. It is not ours.
By steamer we came to the cave of the Revelation
    where a boy is blowing bubble gum
    in the yellow air by the candles.
Is this the end? We lose and we begin, and climb
    nervously. Wind is wild noise.

Sun bakes the white crenellation on the hilltop monastery.
The heavens open and a white horse steps
    on mountains in the water.
Can we see? The daystars fall like figs
    cast down by the windmill gale.
The sea is glass mingled with fire.
Fire in us who love. We lose. We wake.
    On the wharf an octopus, in
    each tentacle a horse of salt
    shining like the seven sister stars.
The dream ends here. Fire in us who lose.
    In the dark cave we see.

Hunting

It is fall
and the Kikuyus are hunting as usual
    on the lion and leopard plateaus.
One captain America finds an oriental solution at My Lai
    by massacring villagers for sport,
while at home the season is open for death.
Farmers and barbers enter the forest
    of brake and partridge swamps,
creep like red ants up the Green Mountains,
raise their great phallus to their shoulders
    and pump fire
at the deer of love.

In high Kenya there is fresh snow
while six bulls die in the afternoon in the ring
of the cheering city of Andalusian Baeza.

With a Rhino by the River

After trekking a few weeks around Annapurna
           under the ice sun,
I bus south down to Nepal's open jungle
and rent an elephant who munches on a small palm tree
as we trudge through villages to the river.
A rhinoceros is torpid
yet when I conceal myself incautiously
behind a banyan tree,
           foolishly downwind,
the rhino signals he isn't envious of my elephant
or my little form in the dawn.
We gaze at each other for a century.
His eyes are cups of green water with Genesis singing
           at the bottom.
Neither of us worry.
I wouldn't scoop weight and armor
           with a bullet.
He doesn't care that I can read and he prefers grass
           to my raw flesh.
I don't covet his tusks sticking into heaven,
even as a Chinese aphrodisiac (booty of recent slaughter).

A decade later I ponder the great myopic beast
looking up from the river plants to glare at me.
He is still the brown knight with elaborate plates
           of Asian armor hanging
beautiful under a root-tasty breeze.
I want him for the adventure of the soul,
for a poem about a rhino charging and goring
           an outsider.
He wants nothing
and lets me stand with him by the river.

Salem Graveyard and Witch-Hanger
Colonel Hathorne

In the graveyard in Shalom (the old name
the Puritans gave Salem in 1626),
in November moonless snow, almost lame
on stumbling ice I wander. Lord, how black
despite the snow! Remembering Anne
I'm looking for Simon Bradstreet. His plaque

stands somewhere. Maybe he's in a fat tomb
among the withered shoots of marble.
But I spot the hanging judge, the first groom
of death and fundamentalist of terror
in America, who chose the fraud and scare
of witchery to burn the nineteen for their error

of being of a race of women. A banal grave man:
Here Lyes Interred Y Body of Col Iohn Hathorne
Esq Aged 76. His great-great-grandson Nathan-
iel Hathorne, age 22, at Bowdoin College, is so
enraged by his judge ancestor he adds a *w*
to his name to become Hawthorne. Now no

way in this slippery light to find Anne Bradstreet.
In the morning? No stone for the woman's bones,
but beer-crazy scary Halloween joy shrieks greet
old witches. Children in witch gowns wait in a row
outside *The Witches' Black Church* beside our inn)
to glimpse the hangman's holocaust in the next show.

Artist by the Hudson

On a mound by the Hudson River an old Polish gent,
    a one-man band, hops around
as if he were a tightrope artist between buildings
    but he's a dwarf and hunched

like a crow on the ground. He's a bouncing hoop.
    It says VLADO on the boom drum
hung low on his back. With each hop his worn eyes
    pop brightly open, he clacks

knee-bells together; then raising his drumstick behind,
    he slams the leather drum, and gold
cymbals explode on leaping boots! The sky responds
    with a division of terrified pigeons

scramming. Vlado stands, blasts his trumpet at a mob
    of kids trailing him, and screams
at squeaky sparrows with no pennies for the artist.
    I don't know him. He must be

an old European street man from another century,
    and shelling out dough
is the job of grownups. In my pocket I've got a nickel
    for buying marbles.

A big shot I toss the coin into his checkered cap.
    I squander my fortune. With a wink
Vlado tips his hat. Now a bankrupt New Yorker,
    I waltz across the meadow,

tooting my harmonica noisy like the grand maestro
    until I trip over a rock, fall flat
and crack a front tooth; then bound up with slow eyes
    bloated with my dirty Polish tears.

Memory House on Plato Street in Junta Years

In the small rented house on Plato street
I stumble through the Greek newspaper,
then stroll through the alleys of Kefissiá
on narrow sidewalks crowded with cars
(the lamp posts have posters with pictures
of leftists in jail or exiled on prison islands)

and descend into a bistro to hear Psaháros
sing us and collapse us into cloud soul.
Smoky but not jammed tonight. He sings
his gravelly *Agonía, agonía.* Earlier I walk alleys
of Thessaloniki, sapphire of the Jewish diaspora
where the Goths put up a wall and gas

seventy thousand Spanish Jews still with keys
from Toledo and the court of Alfonso el Sabio.
Who remembers a slaughter in north Greece
where the ancient inhabitants are stoned
in the central square and trucked away
to special gas trains? Today I straggle among

the dictatorship colonels (they house arrested
Ritsos and Seferis), and in this taverna
where a few couples have finished dancing
to the love songs of Manos Hadjidakis,
I forget, sip retsina near the floor lights,
sit mesmerized by Psaháros singing agony.

Speakeasy 20s

One night in the speakeasy 20s long before
I was born, a formal letter comes
from Giorgio de Chirico and Henry Moore
saying they have selected me
as their melancholy poet and would I let them
fatten me into the mystery
of paint and stone. Fabulous! So Giorgio
paints me as a babbling mystic
dreaming of a building shaped like an O
and Henry sculpts an Olmec head
he fastens to my torso and I agree to pray
for rain. In those days I'm not dead
and hope for eyes and bust my chops to stay
awake to work out the enigma
of the universe before I crash on Monet's hay
stack. In my fantastic room
de Chirico has painted a million windows,
each held open by a magic broom
blossoming into almonds and a saxophone.
Thanks, dear artists of the 20s
for freezing time and me in paint and stone.
Giorgio, Henry, you've banished care
in beautiful illusion. No more aging. The tree
of your elation grows in my despair,
and being a coward I love the Spartan victory
of MOMA art and Russian poets
in their suicide and execution. I shove my knee
against my mouth so I won't squawk
at all you master friends who salvage me in our
speakeasy where I drink your talk.

At My Funeral

I take a seat in the third row
and catch the eulogies. It's sweet
to see old friends, some I don't know.
I wear a tie, good shoes, and greet
a stranger with a kiss. It's bliss
for an insecure guy to hear
deep words. I'll live on them, not miss
a throb, and none of us will fear
the night. There are no tears, no sad
faces, no body or sick word
of God. I sing, have a warm chat
with friends gone sour, wipe away bad
blood. And sweet loves? I tell a bird
to tip them off. Then tip my hat.

I, W.B.

I ride my blue bike to work
down a potted black alley,
a shallow scholar and a minor poet.

In the wire cage I carry
the Song of Songs, my latest love,
and hear the coeds sigh as they screw

in barely furnished pads.
I don't even have a beard
to show. I live a bit on home, a few beers

and what the others tell me.
My soul feeds on foreign flicks
or loneliness, terror, and a flirting pit

of light. A loner among friends,
at night I take a sleeping pill
that wakes me up to dream and dream.

Against W.B.

My friends say to me I talk too much
or show my poems cheaply to anyone
or am still a child.

They couldn't hurt me if they were wrong,
and bats who wander in my sleep
dive at me with me,

my chatter and stunts; all facts and proof
of guilt. And when they tell me, I know
deep down they are right,

down in the belly where the tense child
wants to explore and scream what he feels.
I loudly accuse

my mouth, and say it's time to become
a man. Yet sly I am a man
or a savage child.

New York, a Village of Lovers

In New York everyone has a history. Bosh,
my red cousin, came straight from Stalin land,
skipping down the gangplank in black golosh-
es with a smile. Lucy my nurse—my grand
first love—was French from icy Canada,
a snowflake beauty. Dad flirted, so Mom
hired Leah Scott from English Jamaica.
I sat on Leah's lap when she polished
the silverware, and on her back when she scrubbed
the kitchen floor. When Lucy slipped away,
my princess vanished and it seemed unfair.
I wandered off and sought her evermore
in planes, in trolley cars, on lonely roads.
Even in Mexico she was the air.

Old Man with a Cigarette

When I see an old man walking the street,
troubled by his gray depths, waiting for time
to solve or heal the facts of age, I eat
my tongue and lock my hope. I will not rhyme
his failure and gray hair with mine, and yet
not Sherlock Holmes of Baker Street nor God
of Israel, Rome or Mecca ever let
this fading human win a round. I nod
to him. He doesn't see me cruising by
in my Accord. His eyes fatally soak
up nowhere air. He is grim and alone,
smoldering with his cigarette. Goodbye.
I face a mirror and enjoy my bones
in happy flesh, yet both of us are smoke.

Glistening in Boston

1905 was a good year. Grand world fairs,
forty-two makes of shiny automobiles
for just a few long roads—no thoroughfare,
and Bobby Barnstone was old enough to be
on his own. At twelve some nights he slept
in the freight yards, in alleys, a doorway.

The world before him glistened in Boston
like beer in the nickel lunch saloons
where he ate between long days underground
in the snaky sub where he sold the *Morning
Globe* and the *Evening Globe* and had a team
of boys working for him. He had no longing

for school (he quit in the sixth year of grammar)
or home and a father who belted him around.
He was destined to climb the Eiffel Tower,
drive a spiffy Packard with running boards,
to sleep on a cot in an empty swimming
pool in '41 while sailing back with hordes

of Americans caught by the war in Europe,
all on a jammed liner. No photos of that boy
in Boston, nor of him making his escape
on the *Ile de France* crisscrossing the Atlantic
stippled with German submarines crammed
with torpedoes, back to safe harbor in New York,

nor of the failed silver merchant sprawled
on a Colorado street. Of the man, I remember
enough to love him wildly. I wish I could call
up more. Some shots hang in memory. The wind
has saved a few for me—his gold rimless glasses,
a few silver goblets and a dark pearl stickpin,

the bolts of nightmare and loony dreams—each
a scar of surprise. He doesn't leave. But most
of him is mystery, humming conch shells on a beach
of desolation. He always took my hand.
Right now he's off in the Fayum, conversing
with mummies scheming under Egyptian sand.

Villanelle for Mohammed Azawai, Feeder of Nightingales

When the gold dome blew off the Shrine,
Azawai, crazy about birds,
Fed nightingales to hear them shine.

He owned a pet shop on the line
Between Sunnis and Shias. Words
Of vengeance screamed from every shrine.

Four days he hid indoors, his sign
Of fear. Masked men broke in, blackbirds
When the gold dome blew off the Shrine,

Took him and drilled holes in his skin.
Azawai the spy, they said. Absurd?
His nightingales cried from his shrine.

Small body in a sewer drain,
Hogtied, tortured, his mother heard,
When the gold dome blew off the Shrine.

The meek tenderer of pets lay slain,
His brain blown out. His heart of birds
(When the gold dome blew off the Shrine),
He fed nightingales to hear them shine.

Gabirol's Gazelle Moves into Light

In Zohar (זהר), the Book of Radiance
the eyn sof lies not in black solidity.

Within the concealed mind cave
a black flame issues from the mystery of *Eyn Sof.*

It becomes a fog forming in the unformed
and springs forth into luminosity.

From that God tree of infinite light,
Adam sees from one end to the other of the world

like the eternal gazelle of hill and savanna
to reveal original mystery to the world.

His eyes translate darkness into a bright book
of the architecture of black atoms, green

cries on sexual meadows, and a basket of stars.

مولانا جلال الدین محمد رومی
Rumi and the Bird of Light

In 1207 Jalal al-Din Rumi
is born at Balkh near the Afghan frontier.
He will die in Konia in Byzantine
Rum after a life of seeking—
like 30 pilgrims—the mystical bird.

Only with that bird will he
have power to transform the world. His friend
comes at night, tells him
to eat with his mouth closed.
He hungers, examines the cross, a Hindu

temple, an ancient pagoda,
and finds no trace of the bird. He climbs
the mountain of Kaf. Even
in Mecca there are no wings.
He asks the philosopher Avicenna. No word.

Rumi translates day to night,
life to death, sun to rock, and seeks any way
of converting random love
into a source on meadows
or heaven, even under the desert rocks. As for

human lovers, with whom
he learns the science of ecstasy, he feels empty
and turns his back on them.
With no bird of light
he is impotent. The Sufi poet moves thought

into slow night and opens
his eyes to dark. Yet as a hermit he scarcely
moves. Without light,
he loses hope of translating
the world. His hands hang like lifeless coins

in sagging pockets and he
and the world jam to a halt. Jalal al-Din Rumi
seems dead, but memory
has not ceased. He recalls
how as a child along the Afghan border with China

he witnesses great herds of herons
and flamingos filling the horizon and suddenly
swooping onto the sand
where with literary alchemy
they leave the infinite alphabet of white peace.

Landing on one leg, their claws
turn into fire and melted crystal sand into broken
Chinese ink spelling
an undeciphered ecology
of Asia. The Sufi poet rambles through all fresh

words in the cosmos. He
must carry into Persian verse interior clouds,
butcher shops and gardens.
There remains a single droplet
of low flame in his eyes. In that stillness Rumi

is staring, a disturbed creator,
yet he perceives sparks moving out of black clouds,
camels with lakes below
their humps, pheasant tracks
that print Chinese calligraphy on earth. Floods

drown Mesopotamia dotted
with ravens, ibises and underworlds. Yet how
can he transfer the cosmos
to visible ink? Rayless within,
his ink is black on black, his eyes looking

inward are totally blank.
Rumi turns his head down and sees where he
hasn't gone. Through mist of
vague brain sparks of nowhere
he glares at a bird of light dancing in his lungs.

Winds on the Tableland

You surprised me. I was sleeping on a bag of sand
under poplar trees along the Duero River.
I had wandered on the tableland for three years
and never spoke to the peasants in the taverns
or smoked with the February winds inhabiting my sleeves.

Then you were there.
The reddish walls of the ancient city were not shocked.
The sandtrees and magnolias gave no sign to the winter moon.
The merchant threw out the delinquent mother
and her bony children
while the planet rolled about its pin
as on an ordinary day.

You came. Surprised the air and painted mountains
with windy dictionary stars.
The massive news was a secret I smoked each night in my room
before the ordinary sun struck the tableland.

Bartleby the Scrivener

Bartleby the Scrivener stood all day behind his screen,
staring at the brick wall outside his window
down on Wall Street. Pallid, thin, unseen,

the forlorn copyist preferred not to copy
and left the law office room. Day and night
the former Dead Letter Office clerk sat by

the banister, locked out of his scrivener's dome
until the landlord hustled him up to the Tombs.
There the turnkey gave him the freedom

of a patch of grass and the grubman offered food,
but, preferring to be with kings and counselors,
the silent man refused to dine and soon lay down

on the yard to die. Bartleby is the other side of me,
and the disenchanted copyist was a hero
and a forlorn ascetic who never acquiesced,

yet I would still prefer not to be Bartleby.

from
Tuberculosis in My Lungs

The Big Cat Will Let Me Know How I Am:
My Blood Dyed for Truth

Egyptians, Poe, and Baudelaire love cats.
In Egypt and in *Marvel Comics*, Bast
is Middle Kingdom savior against rats.
Poe and Virginia, freezing in a ghastly
Winter, use Catterina their cat
As a fur blanket. Charles Baudelaire fled
To Brussels to escape the bondsman at
The door, pawns his gold watch, shares milk and bread
With a stray hotel cat. Monday the CAT
Scan will tell MDs how I am. I'll go
Into its belly, my blood dyed with truth
To see my lungs. 'I do not fear the sleuth',
Captain Courageous says. I say I'll know
Tonight how long I'll watch the Yankees bat.

A Sea Ride to Port Unknown

Just wait! In Latin tongues the verb for wait
And hope have equal sense, so I must spare
Despair. I need air. *Despair, despair—spare!*,
Hopkins cries. Gnostics say Eve finds her mate
And kisses him with breath to join tick-tock
earth time. I count the years before I rot.
Adam cashed out. Next day I see a doc,
A pulmonologist who'll check the hot
Iodine in my veins. His imperial take
Will say if I'm to live or disappear
At sea. Just wait! A week to roll and flare
On panna cotta with blueberries float-
ing in my mouth. I'm not prepared to wake
Up dead. Be cunning, Doc. Don't sink my boat.

Before the Trial

Doctor X, you're the mouth of numbered charts.
Tomorrow afternoon at 1 A.M.
You'll be the judge and jury of my farts
And inner parts and sentence me as lamb
For butchering or parolee to mind
My ways, and I sincerely hope you're kind.
You have my records but no mug shot. Sir,
Give a guy waiting for good days a break
Or soft kick. I'm not strong before the blur.
Doktor, I'm not the only patient flake
You help. Soon your verdict. I paint the sun,
Scrawl, do my pushups—all of no import.
If I am guilty, darkness sounds like fun
For creeps. If you spare me, you're a good sport.
Hooray

Hooray

I'm on parole! You spared me with your eyes.
Yes, darkness in my lungs is normal. Soul
Needs gloom to guard its ghostly paradise,
But white is where the killer microbes stroll
And copulate. I've too much white in me.
First doc guessed *Cancer*. Cell devil. You say,
'What d'ya think you have?' I utter, 'TB.'
I'm loyal to poets. 'You're on track. It's a
Cousin of TB, *Mycobacterium*,
The Bird Disease.' So neither asthma nor
the Big C? 'None! Your galaxies shine. Bird
Is not contagious.' I love birds! 'In sum,
In one year you'll have new lungs.' I was the poor
Prodigal son. Now I'm saved by a word.

Verdict, August 1, 2009

I wake for the first time knowing I am
Tubercular. It is an August day
In San Francisco, cold, a summer Sam
Clemens would say was his worst foray
With winter. I'm on four wonderful an-
tibiotics, feel great and a bit pale
With the lung disease of John Keats who lan-
guished in dry warm Rome. The nightingale
Surgeon, through bloodletting and no known cure,
Suffered the body's torments. No return
Of voice. Sun is contradicting Mark Twain,
The camellia trees by the window burn,
The lowly tuber in my chest can't gain
my heart and brain. Day is me the impure.

Can It Be Happening to Me?

Can it be happening to me? No. Yes. Why me?
I'm here as a select, for the first time
On earth, and don't know why I'm fed a tree
Of life. I scarcely know who is this mime
I dwell in as my strolling shade. I'll play
The role and won't ask more. And as for death,
That fool, I'm not Othello killing day
In guilt, nor like my brothers. All is breath!
It's breath that plays with me, and I play back
To win against brutal intruders. Bill,
Calm down. Just take your pills and hit the sack.
I'm young but use old slang—or old and dream
Of better days for blood and pen. Be still,
Be still inside. I look. I'm calm and scheme.

The Hole of My Lungs

Two doctors tell me they see a black hole
Down in the region of my lungs of soul.
John Keats also a doctor sees that space
As a black sky where strange comets are born
As they rumble around choosing a place

To fall. The surgeon Keats suffers the worst, forlorn
Enough soul-flashing self-pity. I'm okay,
Complete recovery if I'm pill wise
And no all-nighter stints and don't betray
The liver by neglecting the cheap prize

Pill, vitamin B6. The liver? Where
Is it? Below your ribs, lower right side,
The pulmonologist confides. Liver?
Like *lifer*, O to keep her as my bride!
She is my golden triangle. Big as

A football, she detoxifies, makes bile,
She breaks down cells, secretes. The hepar has
The powers to self-generate. Maltreat her,
Comes hepatitis. Grand Promethean smile,
She's fire. I'm not a dier but a liver.

Bonjour Consumption

Bonjour consumption, good morning sunshine.
Mad cells, how are you in your pillared state?
I break your knives and forks since you would dine
On me. No place at table for an ingrate
Who joins my body warmth and tries to kill
The host in hostile takeover. Consume
Me for your snack? I've caught you. You can chill

Out elsewhere. This body's a snob. No room
For parasites. *Bonjour tristesse, adieu
tristesse. Hit the road Jack, and don't 'cha come back,
no more, no more, no more!* You make me laugh
And cry. Fuck you! I'm losing it. You track
Me and attack. Posturing golden calf,
You fail, you fall. Drop dead, *adieu monsieur.*

Ghetto

I'm in the ghetto of malignant cells
With whom I am at war. I spit to see
And gauge if they are dead or ring mad bells,
The clangor of the bells in the belfry
And tunnels of my lungs. I'm a machine
Contending with machines I think I'll beat,
I think. Sometimes my bravado is lean
Because the violin filling the street
In Paris was for coins wrapped in a crunch
Of newspaper. That morning tune comes from
A Picasso woman, her hand holding
Her blue iron. Enough bathos. I bunch
My weariness back in a jar. The drum
Of silent battle. Bacteria don't sing.

Gullible's Travels In Fog Time

I put on a good front before each friend
And me the gullible who needs to think,
Don't cry for me. My state doesn't commend
A wooden tear, an iron dime, a wink
Or shiver of the soul. Go find a stage

To waste the bottles of your sympathy.
It's true I lie, yet my mendacious cage
Is good while I am under lock and key.
The London fog was once my comrade in
Our Chelsea flat. Fog's now in me. I feel
Nostalgia for the noxious smog, that fume
That killed the exhibition bulls. A pin
Of memory warms this icy blooded eel
Slinking through sewers, loving the gloom.

In the Open Air I Am No Danger—Indoors I Am the Plague

Typhoid Mary denied, went mad, spread death.
I plough the fields of hope and hold my breath.
Pierre Grange, 'Mary and the Beast.'

Weary and sick I'm fascinated by
The mysteries of disease. News of TB
Enlightens as it frightens in a sky
Of changes. Yes, I sleep and suddenly
I eat prodigiously. Bugs keep my weight
In tow. Weary with circles of boom pills,
C'est trop, too much info. It is my fate
To know the real, not metaphysical,
Terror of fast goodbye. Here at the farm-
ers market, Friday's romp, I nod and smile
But *keep my distance*. Hamlet loved to spiel
With clowns and actors. My Italian pal
The orchid man and I we flirt with harm,
He for a girl, I with what I don't reveal.

Cool Mountain Air

Cool mountain air. After I got TB
in Zanzibar or Kenya, I look for
Mann's magic mountain and climb the Andes,
trek around Annapurna, watch the soar
of eagles skim Morocco's Atlas peaks
and float to far Kilimanjaro snow
warming, melting. Grand mountain writers like
Montale and Montaigne ponder and blow
Tibetan winds at me. With my scarred lungs
I ramble Oakland Hills—our glowing Alps—
a mound of humble clowns who spit at death,
who dance up sky-high ropes to risk their scalps
for crazy crowds, and scare me laughing young.

Sun the Eyelid of the Morning

The eyelid of the morning fills with sky.
Light gladdens those born into misery
Who thrive and scorn the jackal sleep with kings
Of night. I'm a free street hound. No death fry
Of germs is circling in my blood. The grass
Swells the belly of a firmament young
With daybreak noise, and sunrays craze the glass
Of heaven, brightening stars away. I long
To dump depression in a ditch. My talk
And tongue suppress the taste of poisoned phlegm,
And like the metaphysics of my walk
My friends pump joy in me, claiming I am.

Letter to the Bounteous Earth

From your carbons and oceans you form me,
A human with a name and brain to write
This thank you note. I breathe a ton, am free
To see and be this puzzle in the light.
I own no house, enjoy the poverty
Of an old bohemian. I delight
In books and talk, raw trips below the sea
Of mind to find another me, a flight
Inside to spot pins of eternity
Where no death walks, where sun illumines night.
Though heartbreak in the African fever tree
Spreads in my darkness and I cannot fight,
On this bad day the bounteous earth must be
A friend. I breathe and watch the landscape write.

To John Keats (1795–1821)

The saddest verse you write begins, 'When I
have fears that I may cease to be.' With no
Alchemic drink to spare you from the sky
Of starless black or opera lens to slow
And glamorize the malady, you share
The pestilence of Brontë and Balzac,
Of Modigliani, Orwell, and Molière.
I'm in your club, but not your death. This sack
Of killer germs I drug, obscuring fear
And my ink burns. How will you pay your trip
To Port Unknown? To friend Severn you say,
Lift me up, I am dying. I shall die easy.
Don't be frightened! Thank God it has come.
Before the dawn at four comes your black ship.

Last Letter from Albert Camus

Camus got TB early. I hit eighty
when it sneaks in from Africa, my lungs collapse,

I dance tangos to spite the crap in me.
While soldiering in France, I read Camus

any time I can. Once I recall Taps,
clouds falling. Even the one-armed French med-

ical captain snaps a heart-felt salute,
the bugle grabs my sentimental head.

We exchanged letters just before he died.
Camus loved Machado. War the brute

killed Antonio, a fast car Albert; *La rue
d'Alger*, lampposts and street singers cried.

Dew Is the Kiss of Daybreak

Dew is the kiss of daybreak. Mystics wake
And eat old bread and larks assemble in
Their lungs to drown out noisy cares and make
The pestilence of sickness yield to win
The sun, a cottage in the blackest sky
Of heart. Dew is the mix of spit shared by
True lovers on their tongues. The dew is love
Astonishing the bull. Temperate, sane
Pliny claims dew is the saliva of
The stars. I listen to a FedEx night plane
Rumble the heavens with gossipy mail,
Saying the smoke and wars are here to stay.
I hope to say *Farewell, TB*. You've been
Exciting company: Rocinante
Trotting in my chest with his knight in mail.
Knight, fade like dew and don't drop in again.

Eloping with Young France

There is no end. These pages found their germ
In a rough germ that made my chest a lab
For doctors and a Chinese nurse. The term?
Get lost, they've cured me. I buy a black lab,
Sail north to the tundra free of bugs where
TB rags are lost mirage. *Adieu, mon coeur.*
I've gone to school in you. If I have mates
With me till now, *Bonjour.* Let's break some plates.
Soon the waters over the sky will sway
Autumn. Living in two worlds I elope
With *la jeune* France and sit in a café
In Paris, '48. Wish I could tear
Up years. We all were young and had no fear.
All night I pound new bells of crazy hope.

Miguel Hernández and Antonio Machado Left with TB

My best friends died before I was. But they
Wake me almost every evening. Tonight
I talk with young Miguel Hernández. His ray
Of darkness looks at cockroaches and light
Of paper dolls he cuts out for his son
While he sags in fresh tubercular milk
Coughed out in his jail cell that has no sun.
He's dead at thirty-one but I still drink
From his deep cup and far Machado snow.
Miguel and don Antonio. We talk
Till dawn. They save me and I steal their blur,
Their heart, their skill. 'Enough', friends tell me. 'No.
Don't rob their tombs.' How happy when I walk,
Robbing Machado and Miguel. Then we occur.

Chekhov and Kafka

Each with a Slavic name and no joy ride
Is always holy to unholy me.
I turn to them and they hit me wide-eyed.
They're fresh pancakes. Both die off with TB,
A soulful bond, I'm in their club, but they
Have no antibiotics. Chekhov's dad
Is born a serf, Kafka's a Jew. Their stay
On earth is two doves doomed like Shahrazad
To tell a tale until she's killed. Chekhov
And Tolstoy hobnob in Yalta. So Anton
Rose higher than Franz. Bah. Their thinking hands
Give us refuge. They bale me out with love,
Whether I'm up or down, Anton and Franz
Keep popping tales that shiver like the sun.

Chekhov Walking Across Russia to Siberia

Chekhov, you know sorrow, dying young
soon after walking a year across Russia to Siberia
to help sick prisoners in the camps. Among
them you give the melancholy in dystopia
a mellow reprieve of the sick and damned.
When biology damns you in a German spa
at Badenweiler in the Black Forest,
you say, *Ich denke . . . Ich sterbe*, I think . . . I die.
The doctor pours you a glass of champagne.
You drain it, turn on your side peacefully
and leave. Definitive doctor of mercy
you tend the hungry poor who have no sky.

Bon Voyage

To die is not a miracle
and no achievement. It's a blot
on each flash on our rolling ball,
a lump that's not wiped out like snot.
Am going to no better place
or worse. Death has no kind of face.
I sit alive in our midnight
kitchen, jiggling words to spell
black thought. Shall I find a good light
of clarity? Say farewell hell?
Do I suppress yet tremble fear?
Will reason help me? I leave sense,
abandon hope. Yet beauty's here
and now. Hooray for ignorance!

Consuming Tons of Air Is Good

Consumption doesn't worry me. I like
To watch it fade. I'm short of breath but when
Antibiotic time is done, I'll hike
Consuming tons of air up hills again.
The blows I gave my bean, will they exact
Revenge and turn up nasty God knows where?
They'll punch me out and hurl a final whack
To floor me. Don't come near with au revoir.
The tumble gave me words. Sometimes I say
It's worth it, but I can't be crazy all
My life. I'd like this book to end. Then flee
By hyping sales, goddamn it, paint or call
On Africa or work on ecstasy,
And feel these demon bumps turn soft as hay.

Making Peace

'Soon I shall plunge into tenebrous cold',
Writes Baudelaire in *Chant d'Automne*. Soon
I shall plunge into TB-free air, bold
A bit at having beaten back the goon
Of death—time's hood—and his coughing bacteria.
Always with me, dark singing Baudelaire,
His blind man gazing tilted at sky air,
His genial spleen. Germ free, heaving a feria
Of wildly flowery trumpets, blue trombones,
And married to a passionate song sheet
To slow time's coup d'état, I flirt with her,
La belle dame sans merci. Yes, she will cheat
Me too, but she's uneasy. Peace a blur,
Too much fire. Let peace land in my bones.

Adieu, Tuberculosis, My Horrible Companion

*Goodnight, sweet Prince. And flights of angels sing
thee to thy rest.* In risk of night you came,
A far train shook me out of sleep, howling
In my Best Western bed. Nothing could tame
You in old days. You choked Chopin to death.
Playing with me, you caught me on the hills
I climbed. You mushroomed lungs and dimmed my breath,
But I benigned you with a fist of pills.
Bonjour, I said. 'Kindly abandon me.'
The time of unicorns, the price of Araby,
Is ours. You tortured Chopin into hell.
Adieu, I do not wish you well. I won
My days. Let science kill you in the sun.

Dry Brush Portrait

I love to think and breathe. A breath
is honey of the Song of Songs,
deer on a hill. Missing these is death.
For now the meal of life belongs
to me. Because I had TB
breathing is dancing elegance.

Hello, London and Friends at SOAS

Even in London and dark poison smog,
Between drizzles I like to walk in sun
And count my friends and with the poets jog
Along the Thames to catch the Cockney puns
Or Macbeth's holler far as the Isle of Skye
And Inner Hebrides. The sun goes where
There's life, even sunk in the soggy sky
Of human lungs. Today, as if *All Clear!*
Had just rung out, the nurse says you will live
Tomorrow, so forget the hearse, you're clean,
The X-ray of your right lung negative
Except for scarring. Goodbye to old Dance
Of Death who beckons kings and cocks, the mean
And kind, to wear the same headdress of trance
And shade. Blake comes for tea with his bright key
That opens every coffin & sets us free.

Overheard

1

A child is a
sleeping good poem
the sun is in
the sleeping eyes
of a child all
good things in the
sun fill a child

2

I want to live
I want to die
love is want to
live no love is
death I want I
am alone I am
I want to love

3

thirst the body
needs water the
heart needs blood my
heart is a well
it wants more blood
to live is to
thirst for water

4

my life who cares?
I care yet want
a you not me
to care the dog
sleeps the day
I live all life
and care and you?

5

time is a drug
it is always
now yet it kills
I can almost
not stand time it
is pain the sin
of nature death

6

all day I think
just me here here
thinking now I
sleep and still dream
it means I am
the blue hill is
I want to stay

7

I hate my self
with some love and
guilt a hot day
falls on my hair
if I can I
will love your face
body and mind

8

I must die and
not know why life
fell on me it
is a cheap black
trick it makes me
try to outsmart
the dark dark dark

9

I was weak but
so was a child
I did not know
and waited time
is hitting me
they say I look
young time is strong

10

I must if a
spoon can drink all
the yellow sun
I must not wait
for light to come
the dark is deep
and full of sun

11

I don't sleep
I gulp a pill
when I don't think
I am just gone
when I dug holes
in Mexico
there was hope hope

12

I don't know when
I lie I mean
the deep secret
untruth I go
about in a
sane face and it
means I am mad

13

if you were more
I would be glad
bliss would be here
if you not me
or truthfully
we were more the
hill O the hill!

14

one life it is
bitter one life
I am not the first
but some had God
if I were full
I could die but
then I should live

15

please yet who are
you? before when
I ask please say
a word please you
must understand
in the dumb mind
a word is hope

16

I lost my tongue
one year and found
the hollow space
which almost made
me free of me
with no flesh I
was wholly lost

17
when my back broke
the doctor came
like stars to a
sailor a sweet
wind the bed broke
and only a
strong broom was good

18
coffee is my pot
it floats the big
expanding dome
the sides fly out
breakfast slips fast
like a dogwood
far stretching far

19
the six selves of
me slip over
each other and
I am so dry
with sneaky nights
the peace of death
is almost good

20
you are like me
that is one good
one good bit of
life if you are
poor like me we
are two we are
a lonely mass

21
how can no one
know but the face
of easy group
doctrine? how can
no you I have
a clue why we
are? no one know?

22
some give up but
most never come
to the question
I am tortured
like an old Jew
in a camp he
knows O please wait

23
no I can wait
and if death strikes
I won't believe
it I always
said yes there will
come a fire peace
a word a love

24
I am not bored
but dull at times
and hot and like
a child who can't
wait for a toy
bored like a frog
hopping a beast

25
when the beast rang
the monastery
big bell I jumped
and ate black bread
and read two nights
and sang sang poor
poor O but loud!

26
the polka dots
fell like a dog
when a steak sits
in its pan my
robe held in a
nude body she
sailed on a room

27
three candles sat
and laughed at me
my toes froze heart
choked in the pipes
the city was bad
in every street
I ran I ran!

28
alone but a
fly keeps the jazz
band loud and loud
it hits a bulb
I smash my eyes
in filaments
fly you are bright

29
slowly I learn
about screws paint
typing yet dawn
bangs in on deaf
sleeping ears one
day I may wake
am I a fool?

30
I know pain it
comes making me
more alone more
then it is hard
not to sleep not
to sleep and sleep
a weak bad bed

31
spring is no one
can say no a
woman is like
a spring lovely
sometimes if a
beautiful thing
is yes it is

32
I sank lay on
silver paper
toy wrecked when
my child woke up
to kiss me what
shame joy I lay
high on a flag

33
the man who was
in this head was
not in one place
I don't know the
exact spot can't
find him I talk
look am I? where?

34
the tongue is part
of the head but
it goes like a
self-winding watch
I watch it flap
back with its own
words I am far!

35
food goes inside
oxygen comes in
I drive a car
the body works
it works wrong the
dark is so dark
food but no light

36
I trace it may-
be a worm birds
now break the dawn
dawn is outside
O birds the quiet
of your loud cry
miracles almost

37
the birds are mad
weep weep weep no
they are birds dawn
my knees are tight
if the pen dries
I can sleep no
the birds are mad

38
I would pay but
how my soul talks
but so what no
god makes it a
good buy before
I leave maybe
the soul will burn

39
I am poor how
can you or I
be fully glad
a second may
be enough one
kiss light fire head
we are still poor

40
yes it is good
to breathe and how
bad because I
know I will stop
can any light be
strong enough to
help for the dark?

41
light is in hell
but just as strong
as concrete love
is it is just
as clear as day
love asleep
in the next room

42
the word is deep
it makes me sweat
daydream stay up
all night drink hot
milk bouillon pills
is there I'm not
mad but deep close

43
is it worth it?
I can choose it
chose to shoot me
with breath I see
a face and know
good eyes I can't
choose we are here

44
my tricks I play
because I can't
give up death draws
me it is strong
my tricks save the
sky a horse white
as salt shakes me

45
in this town in
this life I made
my bed if I
scream it is in
this room honey lands
are there I'm here
with a scream now

46
if I don't stop if
I don't dream if
light is not my
harbor if I
won't pick up the
hammer and club
my brain I stop

47
a sweet woman
is she's not fake
her breasts and groin
are sweet she is
on earth she loves
me and I her
she is I hope

48
the sun is so
deeply good sun
is so good and
day is now I
walk I fear but
O I know day
the sun I love

49
I feel your flesh
warm and funny
as a herring
you ride a bike
I ski slam the
door I drink you
your flesh is warm

50
Light is in hell
and where dark is
water of pupils
you are light where
I am not I
wait for you who
are enough light

from
Poems from Babel

Yehudi Menuhin Fiddles at Carnegie Hall

Yehudi performs his first solo violin with the San Francisco
Symphony at age seven. Later at Carnegie Hall a photo shows
a pudgy serious boy standing by beaming Bruno Walter. Soon
he is Hollywood tall and glamorously slim, playing for GIs in
Stage Door Canteen and at front playing for Allied soldiers during
WW2. He accompanies Benjamin Britten to the Bergen-Belsen
death camp after its liberation in April 1945. Yehudi (meaning 'the
Jew') performs before 53,000 starving inmate survivors in black
striped bag suits and 13,000 corpses still lying unburied in piles
around the camp. Critics say when Menuhin performs, the voice
of his fiddle resonates with escaped prayer.

I am in my smart maroon Carnegie Hall uniform, selling cokes
up in the highest balcony. Mother and I live a few blocks from the
hall. I'm eleven, pick up a dollar a night and sit through a hundred
performances. Tonight is Yehudi, which for me is as major as the
SS Normandy docking at her lively pier in New York harbor or
FDR fireside chatting on the radio.

After a sizzling performance, the audience is reluctant to abandon
their music temple at 10:15. They clap him back from his curtain
hideout, he plays, they clap him back. Finally, Yehudi tells the
audience, 'This is silly. I'll play until you get tired or I get tired,
and then we'll go home.' The soloist plays till 2:15 A.M. No one
coughs. Not a soul leaves. In my high loft I see it all. The great
fountain of chandelier lights overhead that normally lowers after a
performance is now flaming white and flows out with the crowd.
You can hear its light plashing and bounding like a Russian
dancer onto 57th Street. Then these illuminated waves pour along
the avenues of lower Manhattan. Sirens ascend through grills to
sing along with and taste the rhapsodic river of sound. Tugboats,
sensing trouble, blast their boom around the globe.

A carnival of urban noise joins the concerto: Gershwin's car horns
and trolley bells from *An American in Paris*, Stravinsky's traffic
racket from *Rites of Spring*, and flashes of silence from Cage's *4.33*.
But dominating the musical flood in air and ears is Sir Yehudi's

spirit purifying the city as a gentle torrent of violin ecstasy
waterfalls into New York harbor's gaping mouth.

Harlem Jew and Singing Queen of Sheba

A black Jewish sailor from Harlem knocks on
the translucent glass door and enters Dad's office
down on Maiden Lane. Time is a year before
the war. The sailor missed his ship and needs a
hundred bucks to catch a cheap freighter to end
up with his crew in Hong Kong. Dad's taken by
the sailor's upright gravity and sharp uniform.
He gives him the cash. He doesn't expect to see
him again. A year later Sammy Eldad Ha-
Dani knocks again on the door and hands
my dad a fresh one-hundred dollar bill.
It seemed as likely as finding the fish who
swallowed Solomon's gold ring.

By birth Sammy from Harlem is Ethiopian; by tradition a
descendant of Solomon and the Queen of Sheba. According to
Abyssinian legend, the Jews at night turn into hyenas (*jib*) and
are heard calling each other from peak to peak in the Samien
Mountains. Yet the Falashim have a unique status among this
ancient people, since both they and Haile Selassie, King of Judah,
claim the same forbearers from King Menelik I, King of Axum,
son of Solomon and Sheba. The Sheba queen once ruled over
greater Ethiopia, Eritrea, Somalia, and even Yemen across the Red
Sea. When she visited Solomon in Jerusalem, she came with a
bounty of precious stones, spices and four and a half tons of gold.
Her magnificence and munificence inspired Solomon to order
Hiram, his architect for the new Temple in Jerusalem, to honor
her by constructing an angel with gold wings reaching from wall
to wall. When the Queen of Sheba sang her voice was so melodic
and medicinal, the healed crippled wept with lost joy. Even the

hoopoe, heron, dove, and raven ceased cockling and yodeling to
hear the Sheban archangel chanting Solomon's Song of Songs.

My dad's story about the Ethiopian sailor from Harlem goes
further than encyclopedia information I dig up about Sheba, most
colorful of Solomon's seven hundred wives and three hundred
concubines. I walk into my unlighted bedroom and in the full-
length mirror I see a dim figure: my black face. Once all humans
were black like Sammy, Haile Selassie King of Judah, and the
Queen of the lands of Sheba. Race is fiction. The earliest known
homo sapiens date from a 200,000 year-old African skull found
in Ethiopia. Yet my dream is not archeological or revisionist but
purely musical. I love lyrics and song. If I could dream any dream
it would be to return to biblical eleventh-century Jerusalem, sit
in front seats of an enlightened Royal Theatre on Mount Ophel,
with my dad's sailor friend Sammy Eldad Ha-Dani, King Solomon
and his dad King David, all of us singing along with the famous
Ethiopian queen, a strong contralto, starring in her Amharic
version of *Porgy and Bess.*

Maurice Sendak in the Woods

Today in the woods Maurice Sendak
succumbs. He is nobly with outsiders, with
the young girls performing the children's
opera Brundibar at Teresienstadt—a hoax
to fool visiting drunken Red Cross officials
into thinking the death camp humane. As
a child he sees gangsters plotting below his
bed. His hairy groping uncles and aunts
horrify him in his sickbed. They are the fanciful monsters who
people his books. Brooklyn-born Maurice has enough sorrows
to shock and to make us laugh till it hurts. Self-taught, self-
deprecating, the gay Jewish artist reinvents children's literature. he
draws darkness, evil, sexuality, and brash hilarity on his pages. One
offended lady librarian draws a diaper on tiny boys' penises.

All his life he loves; he idolizes his hairy, indecorous monster
uncles and aunts. From his studio window over the woods he
looks at endless beauty. Despite a stroke and the death of closest
friends, the short man stands on a mountain. His last words fit:
Live, live, live! This artist doesn't beef. Today in Connecticut, .
he is with Mahler, Melville, maples, monsters, and his German
shepherd. He's there in the woods. He loves being forever joined
in day.

Cosmos Comes into Being Through a Word

1

Ancient and modern thinkers look for a single word that contains
everything and nothing. Borges looks everywhere in his seven
brains for the single word to reveal the inner cosmos. Dead end.
But his god of paradox intervenes in a whirlwind to say, 'You my
Shakespeare like myself are many and no one.'

2

God the creator accomplishes the cosmos with *Light*. He has a
thousand names, and so he names himself *HaShem* (הַשֵּׁם), 'the
Word'.

3

Plato makes *Justice* his thematic enigma. His dialogue is a
Confucian call to civic virtue, yet the peak is mystically solitary.
He goes to his cave and fishes out the freed captives from their
bench of shadows, who rush wordless into light and stare blind
and jubilant into the Sun. In the flash of detached blindness is
the effable true form. Plato's *Allegory of the Cave* is a model for
Neoplatonism.

4

Plotinos, the Alexandrian Neoplatonist likes the One who is *All*.
He finds the One when he sees and becomes the inner sun amid

the darkness of nothing. Born in Lycopolis, the 'city of the wolf', he eventually moves to Rome where his disciple Porphyry corrects the nearly blind philosopher's atrocious spelling as he edits his essential *Enneads*. Disdainful of the body, Plotinos refuses to have his portrait painted. 'Why paint an illusion of an illusion?' While to Plotinos the body is an annoying illusion; in the soul resides his singularly non-illusionary word: the 'One'.

5

Quakers define God's light by removing it from the heavens down to earth where it enters us as the *Inner Light*.

6

Though the cosmos comes into being through the word, that word is always and never the same. The word breeds many portentously named sects always and never the same.

7

For John of the Cross, Spanish mystical poet of the Golden Age, the word is a column of nine *nadas*, the nothings, adding up to one *todo*, the *all* in his concrete poem:

nada
nada
nada
nada
nada
nada
nada
nada
nada
¡todo!

Best is John on his obscure stairway where the sun in his heart guides him through his dark city night to a concealed grass sanctuary behind the castle wall. There, John (though he assumes a woman's voice) and lover (who may be God) in windy peace merge in illumination. And there they sleep off the wounds of love.

from *Poems from Babel* 289

For them the word is flesh. The word is light. The word is the summit of love that drops into perfect slumber. The lovers sleep in their own land surrounded by deer feeding on a hill and lilies swaying on a windy mountain of oblivion.

The Eleven Commandments

1

I am the Lord and I brought you out of Egypt, out of the house of slavery. There are other gods. But you have one God. I am I.

2

Make no idols. I am the maker. Those who create art will compete with me. You may worship them and lose me. If you make idols I shall punish your children for three and four generations. If you love me, since I am a lonely God I will care for you for a thousand generations. Love me, obey me. No statues.

3

In argument or court or the market, do not use my name for influence. I am a private God. I intervene when I wish, but you are not me. Do not stand in the pulpit babbling as if you are God. If you pass for me, I will erase you like an idol.

4

Shabbat is mine. I labored to form letters and place them on cloth of black fire in order to read those letters as words and speak creation. I created twice. Once in six days. And then all in one day when I created a garden with Adam and Eve. Two cosmic efforts. Remember what I did. It was for you. Remember that you were a slave in Egypt and I delivered you. Now pause, enjoy, even meditate. I command you to loaf. If you are not lazy and joyful on your day of rest, I will tumble stones on your heads and then you may remember our labors. I have blessed Shabbat.

5

Honor your father and mother who, like me, are your makers.
Dishonor to them is abuse of me. If you honor your father and
mother, they will like you and forget honor and walk with you in
gardens.

6

Do not kill. I kill. Time kills. Disease dismembers and kills.
Do not add to that misery. If someone tries to kill you, whisper
something quickly to me. Unfortunately, I may be absent. I tend
to many and tend to be on line elsewhere. But all my work does
not give you license to own guns or kill. Burn the weapons, big
and small, of killing. Have a good life.

7

Do not sleep with the spouse of another. There are many to sleep
with, including your solitude, which may delight you with never
imagined feasts. The world has a mountain of partners. Why look
for trouble? If your heart is beating with desire, remember me,
your Lord, who has everyone and no one. I stand alone in the sky.

8

Do not steal the shirt of your kin or even of your enemy. Worry
about it, since even I who know all do not distinguish between
stealing and enterprise. Even your prosperity may help if you steal
from your neighbor, and your poverty may help if you steal from
your cousin. Look into the mirror. If you see only two figures,
you and your heart, if your hand does not shiver, forget this
commandment. If you steal and your hand does not shiver, you
are destined for great power.

9

Do not rat. A silent face is diamond. If you rat on friend or enemy,
a circle of smoke will turn you into a rodent, not a hare, but a rat.
Better to be a siren, a singing Josephine who comforts her fellow
mouse folk who live in shadows and pipes, than to rat.

10

from *Poems from Babel* 291

I am the jealous God. You must not be like me. I possess the world, and its people die and wives and husband, slaves and oxen and neighbors all become dust and I possess nothing of them. You will have nothing if you do not learn from death, from the dust maker, since your soul, if you covet the things of others, will turn deadly. You will not look in yourself where you are a sky infinitely deep and with unending aromas. Do not be jealous like me.

11
I am a weary God, who has not been listened to. That may be just, since I have taken to long absences. My plate is empty. Do not quibble whether I have been good or bad, whether my commandments are good or bad, whether I am or am not. If you want a good life, I tell you to listen to my commandments. Or do not listen. And if you cannot listen, hear your soul. It is there, asking you to loaf. And when you have truly seen your soul and believed, and are comforted by its vastly intimate rain forest, enter her and forget me.

Disgrace of Nature in the Périgord

A French-speaking soldier in postwar France, I auction off our aerial supply camp's surplus typewriters, tables, lawnmowers to raise money for a Catholic children's hospital. I bark out the bids. Laughter, noise, applause. On Saturday morning the nuns drive me into the country, through bright air above the Dordogne valley, a sunny and womanly soft meadow of castles and old villages, ducks, geese and foie gras to their newly built hospital. Alone on a blue hillock, it is all glass and captures the sunlight. The young nuns are more than kind and graceful in their white ballet robes. They have easy soul. We climb to the top floor. Morning light passes through tall glass walls and spreads like cotton cloth in the corridors. I go to the wall facing the green brilliance of the Périgord below. Undulating farmland, slow tractors, haystacks in immaculate rows, alcoholic vineyards, discreet groves of silk mulberry, brooding chestnut, slim beech. La douce France. La belle Aquitaine.

In the room are nine girls between seven and ten. At noon they are all sleeping. The nuns like white clouds hover near a child as her breathing weakens on this full morning. Sunlight reaches through glass walls to her bed, sunlight quivers on the sheet drawn near her chin. Cancer is ravaging the children, soon to carry them off, but does not ravage their faces. They are too fresh and young for the savage killer's uncontrolled cells and tumors to deface their faces facing the ceiling of endless skies. Despite their inner turmoil they seem serene. The whole singing light of the sun bathes them in their last days above the ground. On the soft and unfeeling hill, nature has no mercy. The roulette wheel of nature monstrously seizes weakness and turns each victim into double zero. Although a war of light and darkness wages in their bodies, they stare blind, beautiful as a sky jammed and brightened with flamingos, a few with half-opened eyes like the Buddha, still breathing life on their last days above the earth.

Rising Sun

We know the sun will rise again. But what is left of sun in moon only half consoles. As to William Blake's chimney-sweeping children, they wake in darkness. By day the shaved-head sweepers sweep lead-toxic soot from chimney flues until the outdoor sky is dark. Before they grow too tall to fit the flue, they sleep and cannot rise until the priest locks the sweepers up in coffins of black.

We lucky ones believe our sun is good and human. We shall never race into the West. Strangely, my heart is with the great losers. With Bartleby, Billy Budd hanging from the mast, and Wang Wei hermiting on Deep South Mountain where sun is a mirror on mulberry and scholar tree. Constantly, the people shine, never mourning a day's fallen sun. Sun glows inside them, a lamp of fire.

All people shine sharp in their cranky tilt on earth. The losers and the children and those alive in new and old pages keep me in faith to whistle with a chocolate bar, knowing the rising sun is there.

from
Moonbook and Sunbook

The Good Beasts

On the first morning of the moon, in land
under the birds of Ur, before the flood
dirties the memory of a couple banned
from apples and the fatal fire of blood,
Adam and Eve walk in the ghetto park,
circling a tree. They do not know the way
to make their bodies shiver in the spark
of fusion, cannot read or talk, and they
know night and noon, but not the enduring night
of nights that has no noon. Adam and Eve,
good beasts, living the morning of the globe,
are blind, like us, to apocalypse. They probe
the sun, deathray, on the red tree. Its light
rages, illiterate, until they leave.

Gospel of Clouds

On cloudy Sundays clouds are in my heart
as if my brother came, as if the rain
lingered among the mushrooms and the art
of freedom washed into the murder train
or rinsed the *peat bog soldiers* of the camp.
On cloudy Sundays clouds are with Joe Hill.
Last night I dreamt he was alive. The tramp
was mining clouds for thunder. And uphill
into the clouds I feel that time descends,
as if my mother came, as if the moon
were flowering between the thighs of friends
and gave us fire. On Sundays when the swan
of death circles my heart, the cloudy noon
rolls me gaping like dice, though I am gone.

Moon Dropping into Our Secret Dutch Attic, 1943

'I want to be useful or bring enjoyment to all people,
even those I've never met.'

Anne Frank

Moon, you catch oceans, glitter them with sun
you flash out from your face, but I am down
here and see just these attic rays. No one
to slip me from this room. You coat each town
with brilliance, but you keep your body clean,
untouched by smoking death camps far below
your gaze. When you are thin, a safety pin
of sexual light, I grab your beams and sew
them in my pockets. I Anne find a hole
through the closed shutters in my attic. When
night locks me in, I see your drop of bread
and turn it into ink, and your dead soul
is mine. Your brilliance through my oxygen
gives me light hope, before I join the dead.

Poètes dans la lune

Le soleil sans mots lance la lumière
qui éclaire le suave air et la chaleur
pour Eve et Adam. Puis tremblant de peur
ils jouissent en fabriquant nos pères
et meurent. Mais les poètes qu'on aime
dans la lune, je les entends sous l'arche
d'un obscur brouillard sauvage où ils sèment
mon âme avec la douce nuit qui marche.

Poets in the Moon

The wordless sun launches a light
flaring out with delicious air and heat
for Eve and Adam. Shivering with fright,
they love procreating our ancestry,
and die. Yet those poets whom I feed
on in the moon, I hear below the arch
of a somberly wild fog where they seed
the soul with a sweet night on its march.

Silent Friend of Many Distances

The problem with an orange tree in Greece
whose perfume fills the straights between Poros
and hugging Peloponnesos is peace
of beauty—radiating always close—
that never can respond but does its part,
issuing hope to make me live and wreak
me zero blind. The problem with the heart,
a tool of time, is want can never speak.
The problem with the brain is darkness. It
has no inner moon lamp to give it place.
Silent rotating friend, your aloof poise
I love and hate. Like every love, far space
creates intensity yet rains its spit
on us. I rant until I hear your voice.

Blue Shirt Firing Squad Fells the Andalusian Poet

In Andalusia sun wears orange sheets of light
hanging fresh in the woods, but where
is the mare on the sky? Must it be night
for moon to glow? By day she's there,
a sexual memory in Granada, Spain,
for green wind Federico. No,
she is a tombstone where the Blue Shirt Cain
firing squad fells him. An ice rainbow
washes his dawn. And while a cow
lumbers on sky grass, devours a lunar feast
of plants of green felicity,
while a poppy sighs and a spinning beast
and child float in his theater, now
the Spaniard's moon of pain torments the sea.

Spanish Moon in Almuñécar, 1951

Behind our Roman aqueduct back wall
at three A.M., the moon like a yellow
buffoon sings over the gray hills and all
the sugarcane is shining in the campo.
Quinces and mother-of-pearl olive groves
fragrance the clouds. I smell mint and spikenard.
The full moon is dashing up the sky, her glow
is chasing carbines of the Civil Guard.
Moon lights the song trembling behind her eyes.
In a girl's voice, like Homer she sings blind:
Mira, mira la lunita, con su carita empolvá.
Guards drape killed bodies on the mules. Sick mind
of the Caudillo's fascist years is a
black moon of executions and Church lies.

Paper Moon in Argentina During the Dirty War

Mario and I talk ourselves blue. Guns talk
in Buenos Aires. Mario Kabbalah.
Dirty War. After his lecture we walk
to the Saint James Café with algebra
of mystic John of the Cross. Mario skips through
the numbers. Jesus calls in Galilee
to turn the waters into doves; the Jew
performs his miracles. It is only
a paper moon outside but witness of
the plateless Ford that rounds up seven men
and throws a woman in its trunk. I hear
the woman shriek. No one can help. No love
of miracle or numbers helps. Again
the paper moon observes the disappeared.

With Borges at the Saint James Café, 1975

We take our favorite spot below the mirror
and waning half moon, cold Araucan bowl
holding a sphere of sunlight for the scholar
and insomniac. Earlier in our stroll
from Calle de Maipú to our café,
we hear the nightly bombs. 'We were an hon-
orable city of humble people, and they
survived on courage. All that is gone
with leaders who've gone mad. I'm sad and yet
I still believe in the nation precisely
because it is a chaos.' When we sat
the waiter brought us our hot chocolate.
and toast. 'You love Milton, don't you? Well, he
too had the gift of blindness and liked to chat.'

The Moon Can Never Know, 1952

The moon can never knows she is the moon,
nor sun know he is sun. The minaret
is deaf, the muezzin yells, the faithful swoon
inside the Tangier mosque, and yet
I talk to her, a blue scimitar in
the sharp kef mist smelling over the city.
I am young in these Kasbah days. My sin
is deep as smiling whores, but don't pity
any Billy. He's stressed, but doesn't know
remorse. Can the moon feel guilt? No,
she's faithful and she never lets me down,
and though far, dumb, a body of dead stone,
I love and crave her. She is beautiful
and her kohl-painted eyelid winks me full.

Lovely French Countess Guillemette in Tangier's Kasbah

The most thrilling moon is in the Kasbah.
I make my oatmeal supper on the gas
burner. Then sleep. Rats in my shoes are ga-
ga, sleeping till the dawn muezzin jazz
fills the neighborhood sky with calls to prayer.
I get up with the rats and swallows in
the roof, and roam through kef down the sun-glare
coast of Africa. Tangier knows no sin.
My French countess asks me to go for tea
and lavish cakes at a Berber's retreat.
'Are you with Christ?' she pops. 'No, I'm a Jew.'
'You killed our lord!' 'No way! He's a Jew too.'
'Never heard that before.' Suddenly,
the glad moon floods us kissing in the street.

The Moon Has Poppies in Her Mouth

The moon has poppies in her mouth
and hippos in her lungs. She glows
in Indiana. In the south
of Europe, wrestler Plato knows
that music lends the cosmos soul.
Moon hills cry silence. I invent
her wordless tune. In bed I roll
and roll, seeking the moon who lent
me unheard song. A zoo of ears
on earth listens while silence sings.
Our earthly makers Cole Porter
and Ravel swoon in reverie,
Johannes Brahms in ecstasy.
The mute moon flaps her angel wings.

In Hawthorne's Room of Echoes, 1947

At Bowdoin College where H. Longfellow
and N. Hathorne were pals, Nathaniel changed
his name to Hawthorne to cut the shadow
and hang-rope of his Puritan deranged
great-great-grandfather Judge Hathorne who hung
the Salem heretics, or so he called
them. I live in Hawthorne's room, up a rung
of worn stairs, second floor in Hawthorne Hall.
Ancestral fame was no help when young bards
Henry and Nathaniel were playing cards
for a jug of red wine, were caught, expelled,
and readmitted. At home they got hell.
In Hawthorne's room their snows sing in my veins;
their woods and haunted moon hum in my brain.

Below the Tuberculosis Sanatorium Above Athens, 1949

Men holding arms in bathrobes like to stroll
from marble Mount Penteli down the slope
to the olive tree zone near my house. All
have tuberculosis. Sometimes they smoke
Papastrátos 1. Quietly, in light
autumn clothes, they converse. I walk
with them. There is no cure yet but slow time
and sun and rest, and then good luck.
At the king's school I cross the German queen
about the rebels killed in camps. She frowns
but lends me books. Soon I'm expelled. 'You're free',
the men in pajamas say. I leave my town
for winter Mykonos. Moon beneath my sneak-
ers, with my sick friends we stroll the lone sea.

Priests Are Nailing Her in Place

The moon is sick. I fear she'll die
    from lack of love, from poverty
    and homelessness. Lost in the sky

our daughter's dropping down the sea
    of negligence. And who will glow
    on walkers in the night? The moon

will show and nobody will know
    because she is a black balloon
    and can't be seen. She hasn't gone.

Yet scholars say, 'She went. She was
    an obscure custom of a race
    of fools.' The moon is sick, and on

her crackled face, a pox, a buzz
  of priests are nailing her in place,
  but moon repairs herself with cosmic glue

and floats to show her throat in Italy.
  There painted by Sandro Botticelli
  she rises lily thin in her white shoe.

Fading Back to Our Polish Shtetl and Black Hats

The spring is late this year. Its winds are raw,
aching a bit. The moon is full. I pad
down through the gully to Salt Creek. The law
of seasons will prevail, ending the sad-
ness of dead grass, and soon my winter in
the barn will end. I fade lonely in space
back to my roots next door to a Ukraine
of vast jade fields and to that other race
inside their ghetto villages. Black hats
and books in velvet. My ancestors? Gone
a century, that blood was me. I pass
today. Since grass can't know it is the grass,
I spot no wings of mystic chariots,
yet in my blood the moon burns on and on.

A Kid Making It with the Hudson Moon Who Is a Savvy Dame, 1939

When I run home into the polar wind
booming along the street, the moon is calm
and almost still, a yellow peach who sinned
naked and lusciously over the lamb
of gully snow. She stands perfect above
the Hudson River, her vagina warm
as the fat taxis where the dopes in love
make out, speeding along the Drive. No harm,
I think, and Eliot can prove those odd-
balls grab each other's tits and prick. No one
can look inside, except the wind that blew
near by. I heave onto my bed, my rod
is steel, my eyes a mess of fire and fun.
That sky lady in the sky I kiss her blue.

Dylan Looks Great, 1953

Dylan looks younger than his beer-fat years,
the master of delight. Sitting just rows
from *Under Milkwood*, I hear every sphere
of Welsh babble roll from the bawdy glow
and echo of his lips. These are his last
utterances to a crowd. I leave the room
for glassy mist on 92nd, pass
from Y to Central Park night freeze. Moon gloom
breaks through high wool. In the Village downtown
Dylan picks up his jigger till the roar-
ing lad fans out. Saint Vincent's. No one's guessed
Thomas was to write a grand opera for
Stravinsky. Dylan is a diabet-
ic. Docs give him wrong pills. The opera drowns.

I Spinoza, Lens Grinder in the Amsterdam Ghetto, Make the Moon Live

Since sky is our spiritual space, I wish
to merge in space and keep the moon alive.
She's everywhere and God's left hand. A fish
and planet fill my lens. Though them I dive
into the heart where I can study soul
whose light is numbered rain. Caligula
ordered his slaves to catch the moon and roll
her to his throne. I own that cupola
laughing in heaven and I'm not a nut
or wise man. I just look and she is mine.
My ghetto moon teams with the Sephardim
evoking our old Spain. She feeds me dream
to shape the cosmos. With my pen I cut
the sky through Latin glass for soul to shine.

Full Moon Over a Two-Note Man in Windy South Dakota

Full moon, I am a two-note man. I toot
on high or low. Tonight I'm low in bed,
and low despite the wonder of you, brute
glow ball bounding through the window. Sour lead
winter moon face, last night you stood over
my car racing beyond the exit on
the South Dakota interstate. Earlier,
I walked shivering through night-bleak Vermillion
under your hardware smile. Soon mud, then spring.
I am a funeral bell, low high, a bag
of coffins prancing under your dark lips.
I can't drag up to drink or write. The sting
of mercy pounds in me until I sag
absorbed into your mouth and blazing hips.

Old Orchard Plane and a Sad Black Moon, 1933

When I flew at Old Orchard Beach with Dad,
I was just five. He squeezed me by his side
in a two-wing open cockpit plane. We had
habits of the future moonwalkers, pride
in modern motors, watches of the air
to cart us spinning in the sun. We spun
a spider's nest to catch our fall, to spare
the earth of nutrient blood. But one Sun-
day in bright May, with no chute or balloon
or winged silver clock of heaven, he,
like me in Orange, Mass., leaps through the brute
air of Saint John. I wear a parachute
and pull the cord, but Dad is pure. The sea
of death calms care. He drops, a sad black moon.

The New Moon Rose

The new moon rose, the old moon in her arms.
I am an old moon jogging in the night,
blissfully panting out to strawberry farms.
Jogging isn't a sin. Age is the blight
of nature, yet I'll smooch and dream, a dog
in paradise, pissing on clouds until
I croak. I push the body as I jog,
hoping it won't break up. I'd rather spill,
downed by a busted heart than a soft chair.
No choice. I'm terrified by mind, not death,
as I spot dark inside. Stars came out soon
after a week of rain and gray nightmare
of months. Now racing night thrills me with breath.
When gone I'll spin my laps on a black moon.

Letter to the Moon

I write a letter to the sun
and ask to let it rain for one
more year. And then I write the moon
and ask to let me see her noon
of midnight in a storm of light.
Then star and satellite hit back
with bureaucratic silence black
and total. Then I use Kabal-
lah numbers to get through. No mail
comes out. I hire a nightingale
to sing. I think they'll love it, but
when I lie down and beg, they cut
me off. So I give up. I die
a while. It works. They rain and sigh.

Moon Escape in Egypt

I love the moon and so am slapped in jail,
escape, hunted, and, when the bloodhounds
pick up the scent, I'm caught, held without bail
until a trial for lunacy has found
me guilty of moon love and negligence
of normalcy. I loved the new moon once
in Egypt. I am meeting common-sense
Ibrahim, my grave-robber friend who hunts
antiquity, a patriarch and seer
of marketable beauty, who sells the eye
of the small sphinx. We meet and share a beer.
I buy the moon. Cheap. His two wives are pissed.
Enraged he shoots his pistol at the sky,
but I escape, the moon safe in my fist.

Patient Moon

The moon is not impatient like the son
of man who cleans the lepers, and the eye
around the planet washing her green sun
of midnight on a few whose meadows cry
for sperm, maddens the people of the boats
with milk flaming on rock. Yet even when
she floods a dying child, she never floats
out of her craters with the oxygen
of faith, nor lords us with a vision ray
of crystal heaven. Full and filled with sand,
her face is the death object in the night,
is now and nebulous. While mystery and
the black moon in my head eclipse all light,
she wakes Edison to fix my blurry clay.

Du Fu Recalling Li Bai and His Moon Swan

December night almost freezes us, but
a bowl of wine, the dishes on the floor
in Ming-bright China, keeps our smelly cot-
tage hot with fun. These days when we are poor,
neither of us holds a post. We both failed
the imperial tests. Imagine asking us
how to compose a poem! Your daughter sailed
to Peach Blossom Spring. The black octopus
of hunger strangled her. My head is white
in mourning for my youth. Good Li, you drink
a lot and write a lot. The moon looks on.
We walk outside. I'm turning blue. You fight
the horror of our villages of ink
on fire, while overhead you spot your swan.

Gospel of Light

The moon is natural in the evening. I
cannot be angry at it. And a flute
high on the mountain is the sweetest lie
of separation. And the stench of fruit,
fogging the blasted lots, over the quake
in the Algerian city, joins the dead
who don't smell sweet. Yet in the inner lake
of light, *lake of the heart* as Dante said,
the rays are stronger than the suffering
and rapture of the outer world. To be
inside and be the light is everything
I want. Yet now I live seized by the wall,
those ten walls of the flesh in which I see
pure ignorance, that is, nothing at all.

Sunday Morning in Fascist Spain, 1951

We motorbike through Spain of Isabel
la Católica and Franco *el toro*
de la muerte and iron hand. The belle
of our farm house, the eyes of tomorrow,
is Soledad, who is ten, blond, sigh-eyed,
lovely. Her dad killed *a guardia civil*,
a tricorne hat with leather soul. He fled
and she's an orphan. She lives on the hill
where the Carthaginian cemetery
cabins the poorest of our village. She
hangs out with us. Justo the Gypsy sledge-
hammers the highway black and strums
his sea-guitar carnation white. Our ledge
is Roman pink rhapsodic by March plums.
Andalusia! Most of her grand poets die,
flee, yet Lorca's moon glares in a child's eye.

Sun

Sun is the eye up there. A glaring, black,
impossible to look at fire. It creeps
on insects, under water, in the crack
of falcon cliffs, on fuzzy eggs. It sleeps
on beads of planets strung on cosmic rings.
Its hydrogen explosions warm the flute
of rays poking through moon clouds, and its wings
of morning celebrate the garden fruit
with hymns of life. On gum and cinnamon
and every spice it heats the chlorophyll.
When Galileo looked through flaming glass
for truth, he almost burned. Its miracle
alone makes light, the eye inside, a gas
of yellow worlds and black night without sun.

The Sun Can't Know He Is the Sun

The sun can't know he is the sun, nor light
know she is light. I fall in love
when I am born because I breathe the night
of life, a darkness fading as the dove
of flame feeds me on milk. My mother sighs
and takes me home. Sun gives me air
and time. In such good space I never die
and get to know I am. And I am rare,
the only body holding me. The sun
gives everything: a bed, a book
of spices. When Columbus finds this land,
the Mayas wear the sun but have no gun
against the cross. Sun in my hand
gives free light till he zaps me like a crook.

A Sunny Room at Mount Sinai, 1955

Mount Sinai Hospital. My mother lay
in a good corner room with lots of sun.
The surgeon traced the steps of her death dance.
A soldier then, I'd flown in from France
where in Périgueux's children's ward, one day
I saw a young girl in a coma. Sun
came through glass walls; the child was beautiful,
her face freshened with youth. Only inside
the cancer stormed. I saw the nun place wool
soaked in cold alcohol on her. She died
that afternoon. My mother's gown was loose
and she told us the awful things they'd done
when testing her downstairs. I see her eyes
today. She too was fresh and live. Some juice
lay undrunk by her pillow. A surprise
of pain. I left the room and she was gone.

A Pine Tree Talks to Me Under Green Maine

Why did those pancreatic cells gone bad
parade as half your life? It seized the floor
your early death, as you became a nomad
in the last weeks. You laughed as you left shore
on the Greek liner floating you to Greece.
Then dehydration on the ship, X-rays
in Athens that revealed the hopelessness,
Paris where I met your tears, a few days
in New York. And you sank from sun. Our blind
authorities of soul copped out—the Lord
and Lady up in heaven sipped their tea.
I came from you. You lived alone and signed
out dignified and patient on the board
that coffined you to Maine to feed a tree.

from *Moonbook and Sunbook* 313

Mother

While you are lowered in the clay
we weep under the summer sun.
The rocking of the coffin done,
our meager party goes away.
You leave so quickly for the night
almost no one on the great earth
observes the moment of your death.
We few who knew your quiet light
try to remember, yet forget,
and neither memory nor talk
will bring you sun once it has set.
Your life was brief—a morning walk.
We whom you loved still feel an O
of horrid absence in Maine snow.

Father Imitating Angels Amid the Colorado Rockies

I wonder what my father thought
climbing the stairway to the door
that opened on the roof. 'I ought
to turn around and calm the roar
of failures and begin again.
It's May in Colorado and
with Van Gogh on my wall I can
make it.' He finds the knob, his hand
wavers. No, he was very drunk
with pain, his eyes were gone, he had
the smile of the detached. In May
we all got lost and he had sunk
to punishment. In sun my dad
ghosted to the edge and flew away.

London Morning

Someone loves me and I love her.
Let every bell in London toll
loud the news. Grief cannot prosper
while we sleep arm in arm and bowl
the moon-sick morning sun across
her mother city, lighting rags
and riches with her rays that toss
us out of bed, that boss the stags
and jaguars on the pampas, clean
eyelids of ocean bubbles in-
to union with huge hugging waves.
Love waits darkly while postmen lean
against the snow to bring the sin
of joy and wake the blind. Sun saves.

Sunjoy by the Blue Monastery on the White Cycladic Island

I like to slap my body on the sand
and fry exultantly as much as I
can bear. Eyes closed I feel a laughing hand
on me. Gold beach. Greek island. Solstice sky.
I love to stroll the surf edge to the near
blue monastery, *Agios Sostis*, sit
on huge boulders, stare out at *Voos*, the Steer,
lonely rock beast bright on the sea. I eat
tomatoes, bread and grapes. No pain today.
One year I live in a stone house made of
fat cubes of sun. Iceberg isle. Architect
is whitewash. Jasmines raise the night. Sunday
brings watermelon pyramids. Above
the quay, gulls, briny wind. Sun is perfect.

Starting in Paris, 1948

It is a beautiful day. The sun blows shiny
on the magnolia. The rhododendron
near Annapurna glows with laughter, tiny
rose eyes below the mountain snow horizon
as we trek at breathless heights. At the lodge,
freezing, we eat scraps in stinging smoke-
air by the fire. I think back to my dodge
with crime in Paris. First night, a bad joke
when the maid nabs my trousers from my grip.
Down at the zinc bar, in my French beret,
I take two hardboiled eggs, order cognac
and black coffee. Rapture! There on my back
at l'Hôtel Vert I can't guess I will trip
around the globe my typhoid-Mary way.

Pamplona Café in the Sun

In an outdoor café off Harvard Square,
I'm sitting in the sun, reading the work
of a black waiter who's asking me where
to sell it. Good luck. I too have had to lurk
outside the store, waiting. My soles are thin,
my hair not bad, yet life is time. The sun
would let me come, but it is boiling in
his photosphere. Back on the square a nun
toots her harmonica, a thin guy sits
against the wall, relaxed. HOMELESS WITH AIDS
his sign reports. He's beautiful. His wits
are sharp, I'm sure. It's time for God, it's time
for God to show. Please show. We all are made
of flesh, yet God or sun can't spare a dime.

Qaddafi's Fresh Sunny Shirt

for Khaled Mattawa

Khaled tells me about his Tripoli
and the ancient sun Phoenicians wrap in parch-
ment and—still hot—dump on the Libyan Sea
where, washing slowly to a Roman arch
over the beach, it lights his mom's backyard.
Her young cousin Qaddafi is proud, lean,
hanging out in the kitchen and quite hard
up. He needs a good coat, nice cuisine,
and a fresh white shirt to wear in the sun
before making a revolution. 'Give
the guy some figs, *couscous*, take him outside,
and scrub away the lice', Mom says. With gun
and sunny shirt, he's sure not to forgive
the king and skip a bloody regicide.

Saint John of the Cross Soars into the Sun

Saint John of the Cross
in his dark night. He sees his lover's face
where no one seems to be. Oblivion
and ecstasy. He sleeps on her. No place,
no time until they wake among the lilies.
Father in his black noon loses his love
of day. The phone terrifies him. Achilles
hugs a vague shade in hell, a phantom of
his father gone forever. When Dad steps
into the dark, like John, he doesn't go
away. We bury him. I can't keep track,
however, since his love haunts me. In snow
high in Tibet we climb the sun. We trek
Nepal. When I am bushed he takes my pack.

from *Moonbook and Sunbook*   317

Happiness of the Patient Traveler

I write a letter to the sun
to shine on us again for one
more life. Then beg him for the time
to let our tongues agree to rhyme
for one more year. And then I ask
for just a day, but he unmasks
me with the alphabet of night,
and when I plead for still more light
he spits on me with hours of rain
which finally washes out the pain
of time. I write a letter to
the sun and say I shall let go
of love. He leads me to a tree
inside, where I will hang and be.

Childhood

Sun has a thousand faces. The steel choir
of Brooklyn Bridge looks over Maiden Lane,
her milkmaid alleys shaded from his fire
most of the day. High buildings. Commerce. Gain
or bankruptcy. We drop a nickel in
the slot and tunnel from the West Side down
to Chambers Street. You read *The Sun*. The din
and clatter stills till we climb up John
Street to cool light. We stroll in sun-fun past
Pildes. I climb a lamppost. You are proud
of us and Pierre Grange watches, your design.
Then one night we go broke. We have a blast
uptown, lodged in a bad hotel on loud
Broadway, and pan for sun in our goldmine.

Buddha

The Buddha sitting on the sun is not
proselytizing but taking a nap.
Earlier, seeking enlightenment, the thought
of his dear wife and child, the palace trap
of comfort almost breaks his will to dump
them all, but gods turn Earth around so he
looks straight ahead. Siddhartha, now grown plump
with canny vision under the Bodhi Tree,
lays his new holiness on sumptuous sun.
The Earth grows dark in spots, a fine eclipse
for voyeurs. When the sun drops to his knees,
the Buddha in his mythic pose is done
with light. Poisoned by meat, death on his lips,
as a bronze statue filled with light he flees.

Car Ferry in Northern Vermont

The car's up front. Overhead, gossipy birds
worry about the ferry in the sun.
Destiny East. I've spent my life on words
although below the sea the words are gone.
Slowly the talk, friends, love born on a hill
become a haze of gulls. Way back. The sky
below the sea is closed even to Gil-
gamesh who cannot undo death. To die
is nature, but the boat is ticking on
into the sun. It's WHITE out there. Sun white!
and our few hours elect eternity
until we dock down in the carless night
below. I sigh for love lost in the sea
although below the sea the dark is gone.

He Was Younger Than Sun

The afternoon my father died
I got a call. The act was done
and never done. I cried and cried
and he was younger than the sun.
Since then, the first death I would know,
time is insane. The fall of Constantinople
is still a blow
today, and though I am not gone
I worry as if it has occurred
already. Maybe it helps that years
confound inside. It's less absurd
than measured separation. Time
is young. My father sighs. His ears
once scarred, he listens for my rhyme.

Be Gentle, Sun

Be gentle, sun. You know no end.
I do. Your memory has a bil-
lion parts. I ask my gentle friend
for time below the sun. The thrill
of light. Or dark of madness or
disease. It matters, but as long
as you persist in me and soar
at dawn, our pact is good. I'm wrong
to ask you, gentle sun. But I
can't choose my love. I came. You were
and are and will be. Dig me deep
with all the light from your glass eye.
Be gentle, sun. I want to sleep
yet also wake. In me occur.

My Father First Saw the Sun on Milk Street

Each child tumbling out on the grass of life—
like the guanaco born in Patagonia—
sees sun, is innocent, and then the knife
cuts free the mother's cord till her pneumonia
drops that child in dark. My father saw
the sun on Milk Street, though his mother paid
his birth with death. Some of us fall to law
of ovens like the spinning lily made
to live a day and then be cast to fire,
and some feel guilt for having kept our sun
alive. I'm innocent, and yet I hurt
since one I loved tumbled from the high wire
between two roofs and bloodied his fresh shirt.
He's here with me, trying to greet his son.

Love Tent

Every few years I dig around and find
a letter from my father with the seal
of some hotel he stopped at, going blind-
ly town to town to make himself a deal
and work his way again back up on top.
It's far ago. I'm just like him. I try
to make time work for me, but time the cop
of death will cuff me as he nabbed him. I'll sigh
and go. The sun on that black Monday will
forget to rise, I'll be holed up in bed
yet scrawl a letter back to him. Dad went
except in me. He takes my hand. I fill
his palm of dust with sun. And we're not dead
because we love and chat in his blue tent.

Don Antonio Machado in Snow, 1939

In the militia truck to the frontier,
Machado and family are fleeing death
from Franco troops. Snow hits his face. A tear
of frozen memory. Antonio's breath
is weak, his chest a fire, and yet he pours
out, 'I have time, I have time.' He has time
eternally. Weeks later in Collioure
he lies in bed. His coat holds a last rhyme
stuffed in his pocket. His clean shirt is white
yet smelling of farewell. *'Merci, madame'*,
his final words. A young man on a stay
in France, he had heard Bergson say, 'I am
amid two times: the clock and dream.' That night
death kills his clock. Antonio dreams away.

'Time on the World Tree'
& Other New Poems

1939

In 1939 Antonio Machado dies in Collioure,
France. Franco drives democracy out of Spain
        and World War II begins.
      I take the elevator ride
upstairs to photo pose with Babe Ruth, an orphan,
who next day goes to the World's Fair to hand
        out big diplomas to
      sandlot orphans. I am a fan

out in the Yankee bleachers with my gooey hotdog.
I see Gehrig. He doesn't speak to Babe who banged
        his wife. Lou nab balls, shoving
      them into his mitt, snares
the impossible. The Babe calls everyone a champ
this year the Germans roll through Poland, kill-
        ing any Jew they can
      drag out of basements with a devil's skill

for murder. Good year for me. Would
be the New York boy scout diving champ. The pool
        up at Columbia stinks
      with chlorine, foul steam. The jewel
of my life comes when I swim out of the crammed tank
to cheers and the gold medal, first and last
        time in life. My dad
      and I haunt the Met. We lapse

in reverie before Rembrandts. Soon will come bad
and good years since my dad has split. He writes,
        and Mom—a peach—and I
      are a great dancing team.
We see Cary Grant in *Gunga Din* and Errol Flynn
in *Dodge City* and Frank Sinatra joins Tommy
        Dorsey's band. In 1939
      how happy we can be.

Can't Beat a Summer with Dad in New York on Your Way Back Up

Summer with Dad in 1939!
We make the rounds of jewelry stores.
Then bowl on Broadway. For school I learn each Latin line
of Caesar's *Gallic Wars*. You teach me how to shave.
After supper we are strolling. The headlines scream:

Nazi Planes Bomb Warsaw! German Armies
Plow into Poland! Stalin Invades from East!
France and England Declare War!

Back in hotel, Dad and I call Mom. She's heard it on the radio.
Supper in old-lady snooty Schrafts.
Then we hit the sack, rise at dawn.
Both of us shave and subway down to Wall Street.
Your office was on Maiden Lane till you went broke.
We save enough to live a week—Great diamond sale!
We peddle precious stones and gold *Pierre Grange* watches
That you designed in Switzerland. Soon all are gone,
but Dad you're back, and there is no third rail
to tempt you. Two guys happy as a whale!

Little Children Dance in Paul Celan's Czernowitz, 1936

Sorrow meticulously skips the air
today. Just a few house bricks see and still
remember splendor. No hint of despair
in prewar days. Young children laugh and thrill
as they learn all the proper dances in
Vienna, capital of taste and pride
in German graces. Girls in silk are spin-
ning on the dance floor; every fancy glide

thrills parents. These enlightened Jews don't fret.
North of the empire Hitler takes his dog
on walks in his Bavarian hills. Celan
lives. Parents not. The grand synagogue
burns. Dancing children die. Au revoir *Swan
Lake*. Polished jackboots teach fine etiquette.

Wisdom in Paris, 1941

Read a philosopher whose work is clear
Cycladic light. The wrestler Plato sings
the death of Socrates who has no fear
as hemlock rises in his limbs. Starlings
plummet. Wittgenstein's aphoristic math
in the *Tractatus* is thought apostasy.
He and Celan make roses glow our path,
and violet rose means violet rose. Yet be
alarmed by Hegel. Jargon ramblers Zen
the brain and cause concussions. You will moan
and die abstract. But love Henri Bergson
for *Laughter* and as a Catholic mystic. When
Germans say the Jew badge he needn't wear,
he wears his Yellow Star for all to stare.

Beatles in Auschwitz-Birkenau, 1967

I take the train to Auschwitz from the white
Kraków of Mongols and Copernicus
to the extermination camp, and night
of nights for souls herded by Brownshirt soulless.
Soon after the war, the train's almost empty.
I step on the rust platform where SS

Schutzstaffel doctor Josef Mengele,
for lined-up Jews, chose barracks or gas shower.
Baby shoes, ovens. Gallows for the unruly.
The ᴀʀʙᴇɪᴛ ᴍᴀᴄʜᴛ ꜰʀᴇɪ gate. I leave the tower-
ing smokestacks, trudge back to the platform. Truly
gruesome. Bored, stunned by time, a workman
drops a coin in the jukebox just above
us: 'Sergeant Pepper's Lonely Heart Club Band'.
The beat's so strong we tap our feet, and kiss
the poisoned air with 'All You Need Is Love'.

Albert Einstein, Wayfarer from Ulm and Bern to Princeton

Einstein thought his biggest blunder was
his dark energy theory. No worry. Why care?
He was right. Wrong was the academic buzz.
'God plays no dice with us. Nature is fair.'

Look at his giggling face and haystack hair.
Besides, who cannot love Einstein
With just a pencil he wrote e=mc^2,
his gravity allowed light no straight line.

He waited a century till a Swiss behemoth
beast with Jobian bones of brass and iron
smashed a Higgs boson and proved his sky.
His cosmic computer was a fiery moth

and while Albert played a hot violin,
his universe expanded endless like a sigh.
Besides, who cannot love Einstein?
Look at his giggling face and haystack hair.

Unholy Trinity

Batter my heart, three-person'd God, Donne wrote:
My troika's *body, mind and time.*
Body wrestles with mind.
Mind yells, Get in your boat
And float us through the creeping crime

Of sun and trickster time. In shocking wind
They wear the body out and kill.
I dupe my being with dawn
And bottle time, vast con-
man soothing us with year and pill.

My friends are battered, stoop, shrink and croak.
This leopard scratches jingles. Blow
Me drinking clouds, not Coke.
Death is a dirty joke.
Time, crack me slow. Don't make me go.

Batter my heart, three-person'd God, Donne wrote:
My troika's *body, mind* and *time.*
Body wrestles with mind.
Mind yells, Get in your boat
And float us through time's creeping crime.

Fate of a Lily

Does a lily go to heaven?
A sunflower and an orphan
drink raindrops for free.

Friend Walt

In perfect health (despite the old TB)
I, now thirty-seven years old, begin
like Walter Whitman. *What belongs to me*
belongs to you. Or am I eighty-seven
and a few days? But we're the same. We want
believers. Great when Oscar Wilde stops by
and you two drink elderberry wine in Camden.
Oscar says, 'I have the kiss of Walt Whitman
still on my lips.' Walt ascends from the moon.
Till the last droplet of day Walt is writing
and rewriting a song, a singular scripture. Jorge Guillén
Charles Baudelaire and everyone we love
spends a lifetime perfecting one good book.
I hope like Walt to work until the dusk
definitively quiets my labor. I won't go willingly.
I'll grab each wink of light and leave
a note saying, 'These words are working
eagerly to belong to you, my friend.'

Daughters of a Cloud

The big rain is metaphor and gossip
as it bounces off the roof

and gutter and congregates in pure atonal
harmony on leaf and flower.

Rain possesses all horizons from soaking
ant to star.

It tangoes around the cosmos, bellows Piazzolla's
majestic bandoneón.

Then out of breath it stops, disappears into the winds
and ocean of oblivion.

Gone like death, it invents silence.
I go to the window

and yes, there is still a Brahms quartet
of droplets

in steady memory. They spring and compose.
The violin and cello are strong.

The rain is metaphor and gossip
and informs:

'Worry pot, be now and do not despair.
We wash the air.

We are water. We make your planet blue
when seen from Mars.'

Pindar says, 'There is a time for water from the sky,
for raindrops, daughters of the cloud.'

Rains says, 'We sing hello. And if morning
brings booming sun,

consider how our thunderstorm and drizzle
launders the earth.'

Metaphysics of Love

For Ted Roethke remembering his line, 'I knew a woman, lovely in her bones.'

There was a woman lovely in her bones.
We danced on melons of eternity.
She taught me secrets of the winter stones
And how a wanderer can think and be.
We took our breakfast on the sighing moon
And calmed her with our heavy silverware.

When forest deer devoured lunar noon,
Good earth allowed us promise everywhere.
We tasted continents like peppermint.
We smelled them, walked them, spouting each new tongue.
Their infinite dark harbors and jasmine inns
Were midnight sun in bed when we were young,

Yet soon I coughed up soul for airport light.
The woman dancing in her bones changed names.
A silly man, unlovely. What a sight!
I fled to darkness where I practiced shame
While time came coloring my hope and hair
Titanium white. I dreamt alone and worked

On the surreal, but thought slept on the chair.
A woman spotted me and wasn't irked.
She saw me as a sterile moon, a man
In mirrored sun he cannot feel; she felt
Me in Tibet freeze weak. Godless I can-
Not count the eyeless years I took to melt.

Surprise. We're happy in poor rented rooms
And get to Greece and France for summer roams.
I love a woman slender in her bones.
We dance on melons of eternity.
She sings the melody of winter stones
And how a wanderer can think and be.

Seamus Heaney on His Death Bed Texted His Wife, 'Noli Timere' (Do Not Be Afraid)

Seamus Heaney (1939–2013)

For me it makes no sense at all to say
that Dunbar, Villon, Heaney in the land
have a new life. I near that unknown day,
I am confused, but my end is the sand,
that dark inpatient ditch, yet feel less fear.
The sleep one cannot wake from still lies far.

In the kitchen a rose struggles. I hear
her beauty (she's the brave one). This red star
comforts me, soft companion as I pass
to midnight trance. My pen's a looking glass
to words below dream ships. My limbs say, Let
us rest. If not hooked on a poem, I'd be

asleep in bed, not squirming till the dawn.
Finally, I pop off and can forget
the pen. Armed with good wine, Seamus was free,
wrote with hot heart. All fear of death was gone.
His bright Irish take at the last door
I envy. He shines. I circle the cold floor.

Poets Are More Than Poets

Every poet is someone else. Mark Strand
is a painter when we are friends at Yale
until the poem overcomes him. The hand
of Dr. Chekhov heals the poor, pens his tales
and plays of drunks and yearning spinsters in
their isolated country homes who'll never reach

Moscow. Gerald Stern, the swift dorsal fin
shark, brandishes his seadog molars on
anti-union thugs in power; his poems pound
with Bible majesty. Painter, doctor,
boxer, aesthete, he makes you someone else.
The grand poet from Alexandria knows

Cleopatra and Antony. He is an historian
of losers, bastards, deviants. Cavafy tells you
of a night in a sordid room in a narrow bed
with his lover, above a noisy tavern.
I spend a month in the Russian monastery
at Mount Athos, reading and rereading

the collected poems of Amherst's Emily
Dickinson and her eternity of selves.
I eat alone, black bread and smoked fish
in a huge empty dining room between
life size photos of the Tsar and the Tsarina.
Dickinson sits there mightily amused.

Who Are the Lyrical Ghosts?

I love John of the Cross, half Jew, half Moor,
the plain verse ecstasy of his black night,
deaf Goya's mad beasts, mad Hölderlin's roar,
drunk cows, and blossoming pathos of James Wright.
We must consider Christopher Smart's cat Jeoffrey.
He is a mixture of gravity and waggery.
For singers with amazing force, you blink

and George Herbert forsakes his cage,
Gerald Stern lashes a sofa to his rainy car
leaving Philadelphia to give it wrapped
in plastic and almost dry to shivering H.D.
home from Egypt and desert Revelation.
Love street poets? Master François Villon
kills a drunken priest in a brawl. In jail

sentenced to hang, he writes *Le Testament*,
his philosophy of questions. Where is Flora,
the lovely Roman, where is Saint Denis
who picked up his decapitated head
and walked six miles while it preached
in Montmartre. Or call on Edith Piaf
The tiny 'Sparrow' sings taller than a giraffe.

Poets Possess Secrets

Poets possess secrets. Secrets are power
that African griots and Asian shamans,
biblical prophets and mystics swim in
on their way to the unknowable ocean
of death, which the Buddha says is now,
and never dies, and others say is heaven
or horrible hell. John of the Cross,
poet of the black night, a converso Jew

who retells Solomon's Songs in sensual
Spiritual Canticles, comes into light
by descending the secret stairway of mind
out to the hidden garden of love. Yeats,
the Lear of plateau verse, infuses Plato
and Madame Blavatsky's rant into
his *Vision*. Visions are secrets revealed
and secrets undisclosed in a book.

To be a poet, be a secret. Say enough
but not the whole vision. No ineffable.
Hart Crane has so many beauty and bell tower
crushing secrets he drowns in the bay.
A child kicking a ball in the street has
the secret. It works. No time to think,
although the same Sumerian ball bounces forever
like a full moon winking amid black clouds.

Miracles for Heroes and a Tear for Slain Goliath

Jesus came walking, laughing on the sea,
the dark sea was foggy but he could jog.
Jonah slept in the whale, with sympathy
for Nineveh starvers like a homeless dog.

He raged, like Job, against his Lord long gone.
Then Shadrach, Meshach and Abednego
danced in the furnace in Babylon,
Daniel in lion cage—no place to go—

pleaded his Lord who quickly saw his fear
and God put the ferocious cat to sleep
and like an angel Daniel snoozed. No moan.

Young David had no weapon but a stone
for his slingshot. Goliath roared at the creep.
Dave cut his head off to thunderclap cheer.

Spinoza in the Ghetto

Sketching in the ghetto, Spinoza smokes,
drinks a Dutch beer. Happiness is a chat
with friends. Enemies? He has none. He jokes
about the seen. His invisible is fat
with stars. Love keeps them spinning, and God who
is everywhere is also infinite
and nothing, just like death which isn't true
to life experience and best forgot.
At forty-three the grinder's sick. The good
is what he calmly wants, and he is good,
his friends affirm. He's swallowed too much dust
from grinding lenses. His lungs aren't clean,
time isn't real, and grim with glassy lust
for God as space, he fingers the unseen.

Rendezvous

Dad, you've come again tonight.
Years since Tibet. Your face is clear,
smiling amid loud trucks. You light
a match. I leave my bed and we're
up in the hills where no one's eye
will catch and denounce us. I would
love to give you my Ipad. You
are modern. Here you need no hood.
Tibetans welcome us. Monks are blue
like you at dying young. They burn
their bodies to protest. You died
also in sadness. Now's our turn
to hike up in the hills. Time holds
you sweet, perfect. To come you've sold
your Colorado home. The messy sky
is grim. Our guide is sun inside.

Odyssey of a Grain

A cook I was not born to be. Friends said
I could burn water. Bowdoin. Find a room,
twelve dollars monthly where I can read and read
through snow-calm night—sad Chekhov and clear Hume.
On a small electric hotplate I make
my oats and a pancake. I am a monk,
my hope is letters on a page. Then take
a small room in Tangier. On a cheap trunk

in the blue Kasbah I boil coffee, eggs,
and porridge on a Bunsen Burner. Clouds
of kef in tight alleys. Walk my legs
off roaming in the Maghreb hills. Loose shrouds
flash Berber girls' enormous eyes. I write
fortified by alchemy of flakes, cocoa,
hot moon on a black plate in Mexico,
our orphans' meal, our visionary light.

A wild west Oakland kitchen. I compose
through night. To make it, I microwave oats
and milk in a Peruvian bowl. Black rose
of memory. Paris rubs her eyes. The boats
along the Seine float coal as workers wake
and prostitutes, mainly old, disappear
in clinics. Opera types down cognac, steak
and grains. Verlaine sops wine in killer beer.

Hear the Chimneysweeper's Ghost

Who is the poet of the poor?
It was a poor man, William Blake
Who wrote of orphan, soldier, whore,
And chimneysweeper boys who break
Their lungs when they are hardly ten
Or twelve, and barely fill the box
They're buried in by older men.
They're gone. No sigh, as if the pox

Had sailed them to a cloud.
The clock ticks for the poor. They need
To eat and steal and hang. The shroud
Becomes their evening gown, since greed
Enslaves them to the screaming streets.
We need you, William Blake, to sing
A siren, pop our ears. Wrath heats
Our globe of forlorn beauty. Bring

Reason into dead eyes. We die,
Little black boy, little white boy.
Our poverty permits no joy.
No sunflower lights a noon-dead sky.
You say, 'I've no sun time to see.
You dropped me, black stone in the sea.
I cry breakfast! Milk, eggs, toast!
I am the chimneysweeper's ghost.'

Be Calm in the Greek Village

Be calm   Be calm. Let winds of worry drop
me down to sun inside, the still light of
a Greek mountain chapel gong when a drop
of still blood proclaims death. A turtledove
floats by the church while neighbors chat. The priest
presses his white gown. Seek peace. The village stirs
and I have lost the need to be the yeast
raising hot bread. I look at the still firs.
They ask for sun, soil, rain. I look into
the library of soul where words are mute,
say nothing. Nothing. Mystic Saint John seeks
nothing. Peace is loud. Sappho picks her lute
of tortoise shell. With stars she knows a true
heart is turmoil. With her I'm with the weak.

You Bequeath Me Industry

Reader, you're real. I must not let you down.
I think of you. I'm safe. You ego me
to be a mensch. We grin. A worried clown,
I love you. You bequeath me industry
of being a fulltime writer at his desk.
If you dump me forever I'll be a mad-
man hiding symptoms. Big deal, yet no risk
since I make you, even the shaven sad
face in the foggy mirror who shows through
as a would-be blur of youth. You surround
me globally and keep my shoulders straight.
But now my solitude yelps stop! I pound
my mind to squeeze you out. You take the bait.
Comrade, you flatter me. I hear you chew!

Borges Defines Happiness During the Dirty War

One evening after reading Kipling to
Borges in Buenos Aires, I took him
slowly downstairs (he had dirt on his shoe
which I wiped off) and out along a dim
back street to the Saint James Café. The war,
the dirty one, was noisy. Gun shots, a bomb
in nearby flats, a midnight visitor
pounding a door, the city's catacomb
of terror operating fine. The mess
and drama thrilled me, though the country bled.
We sat under our gothic mirror and
began to eat and gossip. Borges said,
smiling, 'Reading Kipling is happiness',
and blood shivered in his transparent hand.

The Doublecross

for Giovanni Battista Bazzana
October 16, 2014

Harvard Divinity School has put me up
in Doublecross, a small Hilton hotel on
Washington, not far from the River Charles
and the famed Regatta that makes strong men swoon.
Divinity and Doublecross! These words feed
each other with holiness and Constantine's sword.

I think of Emerson wandering through Borges's
alleys, and my dad born on Milk Street,
who knew these streets after he was tossed out
of his tailor father's flat when he was twelve.
He knew how to get a nickel cold-cuts lunch
at sawdust floor Irish pubs. What street niche

did he sleep in? He sold papers in the subway
T. But most I think of books, books, the great
Common Room at the Boston Public Library,
imitating the Common Room at the Bibliotethèque
Nationale in Paris where Mozart's Don Givovanni
was premiered. But the sweetest literary

memory is the *Bay Psalm Book*, the first book
published in British America (just 20 years
after the Mayflower with 102 English religious
refugees from Holland reached Pilgrim's Rock in Cape Cod):
        The Whole Booke of Psalmes Faithfully
TRANSLATED into ENGLISH from the Hebrew,

a gorgeous moving version, accomplished by
Richard Mather and John Eliot (the latter
the scion of T. S. Eliot, also a religious poet).
The fabled first book was printed in Cambridge,
where tonight I talk about that old Bible. I hope—
if it's bad as this New England-born sinner

might make it—I hope piously that Aztec tomatoes
thrown at my face by the learned public will be
very red, ripe, and delicious on my faulty tongue.
I think of Emerson wandering through Borges's
alleys, and my dad born on Milk Street
who knew these streets after he was tossed out

The Eye-Blinding Ride from Cambridge to Boston

Borges loves the Cambridge streets of Emerson
where the Argentine with blind eyes can spot
the shadows of the Unitarian's flamboyant cape.
We also tramp through Boston. He is my guide.
In that same Boston 24 years later, on first rainy
night of abominable winter, I leave Harvard

after my irreverence at the Divinity School, feeding
on adrenaline. Get out of an Uber cab driven
by an Ethiopian who is lost in circles,
who leaves me in a lot behind our grim hotel
at two A.M., happy, exhausted, but I plan
the next day trip way up to Maine where

I was born as many years ago as Borges lived.
'Go in the back door. Less drunks in the street.'
But there is no back door. We trail down
a dirt and rock path I cannot see, and up
in our room I have lost my vision
in my left eye. In the morning I'll see. No,

it is a stroke in the optic nerve. The blood
clot washes away next afternoon in the Museum
of Fine Arts, and there is more light, but
I cannot read. Now I'm closer to Borges.
Too close. Now a proud Dead-eye Dick pirate,
I dream a dark voyage to kidnap light.

A Lonely Habit

Being is a lonely habit.
My life I spend writing a poem.
The brain is a verse machine.
Most of my life I've been in love.
In the *Paradiso*, love spins the stars.
Our scene is a meadow of violets,
cold haystacks near the Swiss Alps.
Our hideout room is unknown.

Death Be Not Proud

Death be not proud, you hateful punk,
you have but one trick up your sleeve.
Your silent army—like piles of junk
in vacant lots—makes widows grieve
and scares the shit out of strong kings
and sad clowns in your Dance of Death
and antique snows when Villon sings
of ladies now bereft of breath:
Où est Flora la Belle Romaine?
John Donne proclaims that desperate men
will wake eternally: 'Death, thou shalt die',
but death's not live to cry or die
or sleep. Death is a bogus Zen.
I dwell in light while I've a brain.

A Christmas Tale, 1936

On black afternoons we Jews eat tongue,
which sickens me. Before I drop in bed,
I hang my stockings, big ones Howard lent
me for the night; then wake at dawn before
those dumbbells rise and find my Arab tent
bulging with toys. I'm nine. I love the roar
of family fun and never will it end.

Wolf gales zoom over the Hudson River
charge through the Park, ripping up trees and chase
snowballs into my face. But I was born
in Maine where deer flee the frozen space
of her uninhabited forests. New York
seems like hot fudge. I crash into headwinds,
reach our building where the Babe chews pork.

Before next Christmas I'm alone with Mom.
She buys me careful gifts. From five we're down
to three. You grow up fast, Alfred my friend
informs me, when your parents split. I'm mum
out in black snow, dressed like a goofy clown.

A House of Visitations

The last time I see Dad is in New York.
We pass the night talking cot to cot.
He flies to Mexico—a big prop plane—
to regain wife and funds. Finds only pain.

Born a few years before la Belle Époque,
he is a monument till his collapse.
He flies to Colorado Springs. Sad dive
to oblivion. In secret lands we live

in Bhutan where cheerfully we forget
and make his death unreal. But then I wake
and truth sinks joy. In Paris student days

I thrive. Arts, rain. Marry at the *mairie.*
My mom and brother Howard visit me,
stay at Hotel George V. They cheer my trip
to adulthood, warmly advise. A hip

worldly architect, pal of Cartier-Bresson
with whom he does a book on Galveston,
Howie's a tree of confidence. Later
he'll break and follow Dad to the sewer

of suicide. And one more tragedy.
My young brother Roberto comes into being
just months after Dad's jump. In Mexico
D.F. his brilliant youth. My smart hero

hangs himself over the tub. In his way
genius and beautiful, I don't know why
he takes the dark. In Austin a big cheese
and builder. Mom is solid. Water skies

on blue Maine lakes. I love her endlessly.
I love them all. She comes to visit me
south of Granada. Our cheap paradise,
a sun-and-moon casa by Lorca's sea.

Our back wall is a Roman aqueduct.
We walk through sugar fields. Mother is cut
from golden cloth. I never hear her cry,
complain. A cameo. She likes Matisse.

Comes another war. I'm a soldier in France.
War ends. Mom comes to spend winter, off base,
with us. I'm happy as a bug. By time
she lands in Paris she is pale. The slime

of death has got her pancreas. We fly
back to New York and then we taxi by
the Sunday horses, zoo and obelisk
in Central Park. 'My last view', she says.

She's in Mount Sinai hospital. They sew
her up but it's too late. Beauty goes
back to her Maine. We bury her. The day
she lowers in the earth is a black ray

of love the earth can't hog. We all stay on
forever in my brain. We meet each dawn.
Though darkly I may soon trip off, I wish
we all could meet, gossip, and share a dish.

Good Morning, Sister Time

Time is my commander friend. Without her I'm
a ghost. I share each day with sleep
which is a surreal dream I cannot keep
after sun shoots me out of time

in clocks and shops. Often I try to spin
a story song. I've lost some sight
and draw passionately to gather in
faces, beasts, abstract flights of light.

Everything now is beautiful, though full
of my blood gone including you
who haunt me and my pen. You're still in time

because I think. You raid my skull.
I scribble on a page. That's what I do
till I lose time. Time is sublime.

Nostalgia for a Ghost

We speak each night and voyage to the poles
of memory. Mongolia on the plateau.
We speak to sheep in Russian. Our car rolls
around low yurts and no snow mountain knows
you are a ghost and I a dreamer. Swell
to watch the wrestlers. In Frisco we
hang out at the old St Francis Hotel,
eat fish dinners at Bernsteins down the alley
from the square. We drive down to Mexico.
None of this dream. I bring you back. Also
I'm tortured by regret. Ghosts have command.
I pay but who cares? We're together. Night
subdues inspection. Darkly we live light.

Blowup in the Garden of Blue Genesis

Unwillingly blue Genesis makes Eve
our hero. God commands. Eve's a spark
of intuition. She starts to retrieve
our freedom and grow mind in prison park
of Eden where the mammoth rhino lies
with panther, pig, and cranky crow. Eve knows
her body, and Adam goes on to spice
his manhood in her thighs. God sees, blows
up at crass insurrection, Eve gives birth
to mortal children, cosmic thunder tests
their courage, earthquake is a sacrifice
of plains for deadly traps in the new Earth.
Consider how our naked Eve resists
these monster travesties of life outside
their biblical hotel. Now horrified,
Eve invents love and wandering paradise.

Gospels Say

The poor will inherit the earth,
Though one percent are heirs and they
Spoil earth and strip the poor. At birth
Fine children sense their Milky Way
Of cosmic money. Heaven. The poor
Inherit the wind. Zero. Go blow
Your horn. Poor knock on the gold door
And oddballs rise. Great dream. Fellow
Children of poverty are free
To smoke, reside in jail or be
Honorably good. Their angels float
Through smog. The poor and rich must die
Though not at the same speed. Don't gloat.
The poor are happy in their sty.

Rum and Cola

Shall we dance and smoke a Cuban cigar,
drink 'Rum and Coca Cola?' Would be fun
but best to jog these Paris streets as far
as Le Palais Royal. October sun
tastes sweet. With half an eye and half a lung
I am a Piazzolla tango man,
not a blind chair. We all feel young.
Age is illusion. I am alive and dance.
A habit. Knowledge sets us free. The book
redeems. In huge simplicity I look
down in the blur inside and you are there
pushing me onto city streets. I'm less
afraid. Tonight I'll dream bells everywhere.

Tender Is the Night

Milton wrote Paradise when blind. The blind
see best in day when night becomes their float
of images they feel like sonic wind.
Deaf Goya captures a crucified goat,
symbol of the Napoleonic Spain
that feeds his fury. Tender is the night
of hunger common as the starry night
nourishing sand with mushrooms and the taste
of Grand Marnier at two A.M. I take
to drop me into tender sleep. I swore
no more but in the kitchen now I paste
my hope for beauty I might beastlike rake
from Paradise and scribble on the floor

With Borges the Blind Man

Thirty years blind. Finally he can't write by hand.
He signs his books in undeciphered cuneiform
and daylight enters his brain as yellow fog.

Sunday morning, we're strolling to a book store.
By nightfall a taxi strike, too late for buses
so we have to walk, making Borges happy.

It's a bad evening of the Dirty War. We talk
about the savage ambush. Police tipped off,
waiting. Courtyard of corpses. We walk the city

from Palermo to Maipú, from midnight
to daybreak. When the sly one wants to delay
arrival, he sticks his cane in a dim hole

of the broken sidewalk. 'It's like my face,
cracked', he insists. And pivots round it.
'Dim', he says. 'We have no Old English word

like dim in Spanish. Still I keep to my tongue.
Did you ever see one of your outlaws
in action?' I ask. 'Yes, up in Jujuy, near Brazil.

I was very young, and I went up there I guess
for linguistic reasons. I wanted to hear that mix
of Spanish and Portuguese. And a gaucho,

a black man, pulled out a pistol and shot
someone; then slipped his gun in his pocket
like a handkerchief. He kept walking as if

nothing happened.' We near the flat on Maipú
where he jiggles his keys a long time. 'Here
in Buenos Aires, my city, I am lonely. It is my fate.

And so I dream.' The big bedroom, untouched,
was his late mother's. The blind man sleeps
in a tiny room on a cot good for nightmare.

Antonio Machado on a Bench Facing the Sea in Collioure, 1939

When Don Antonio can hardly breathe,
he hobbles slowly to the crumbling sea in France
where now he is a refugee from Axis bombers
whose blasts make Spain seethe with death.
Machado is a memory poet. 1920. Segovia.
The honey-colored Roman aqueduct
snakes through this mountain town.
At one end the Alcazar castle guards the medieval city in the north.

Machado enjoys his gossipy tertulia in the stale casino,
sitting on a frayed horsehair couch with a few
local crony authors or his visiting brother Manolo.

His own pension room is too small to write in,
but his window looks onto a small monastery
where the bones of Saint John of the Cross are interred
in the mystic's last dark night below the garden.
Machado composes poems in the freezing parlor,
a blanket on his lap, a coal brazier to warm his legs,
his cigarette ashes littering his shirt.
He writes draft after draft through the night.
By morning he is asleep, head lying on the table.

That was Segovia and now the civil war.
Lorca is executed in Granada in first days of the rebellion.
Machado barely escapes Franco's blue troops
when frozen after sleepless days and nights he crosses
the snow border at Port Bou to exile in Collioure.
A month earlier Cambridge offered him a chair
but he preferred France where he studied with Henri Bergson
whose time theories undid and remade him too.

Almost a month goes by in this coastal village
where in 1909 Braque and Picasso invent cubism.
He recalls Sevilla and blue days of childhood sun.
He strolls a bit with friends. One morning he walks alone
unsteady to the shore. 'I have time', he says. 'I have time.'

Don Antonio is sitting on a bench facing the winter sea.
He leaves a thousand thoughts on the sand.
Then hobbles back, his chest on fire with disease,
to his Bougnol-Quintana room upstairs and his bed.
He changes to his one clean white shirt.
Madame Quintana the fine landlady attends him,
'*Bonne soirée, Monsieur.*' She readies him for supper,
a last supper. In his sleep Antonio murmurs,
'*¡Adiós, madre, adiós, madre!*' And at three in
the afternoon, she covers him neatly on the bed.

The Camp near Kraków

Auschwitz, 1967

I take a smoky train from Warsaw to Kraków,
The orange city of Copernicus who published books
Only in safe Holland where his new astronomy
Would not send him bound and choking to a burning scaffold.
I switch trains for the death platform of gloom dust
Mingled with blood of ancient peoples.
The three ovens are in the small basement.
They seem to be molded mummy tombs.
Bodies were their fuel for intense fires. Near the ovens
The gas showers. There people screamed and dropped.
The Übermenschen didn't play Polish Chopin on
The piano when they welcomed gypsies, Jews, gays,
And Poles to be murdered. I see the faces on the wall
In staring photographs which have yellowed time.

My Polish cousins died in this pleasure camp.
I look like them. There are no lemon trees
Blooming on the grounds. There is a small
Corner below the roof outside where the unruly
Were each day hanged. One room has a display cabinet
Of tiny children's shoes with no feet in them.
Among the survivors were seven Romanian dwarves,
Tiny musicians and singers. Gas had entered the chamber
When Dr Mengele, the surgeon of aberrations,
Opened the doors, threw water on the Ovitz family
To revive them. Mengele killed only one infant
In his experimental surgery. And they kept their gold teeth.
These barracks were a place of little hope,
Though Anne Frank survived until two weeks
Before liberation when typhus closed her eyes,
Along with composers and bricklayers who lingered
Until their turn came to become ash in the sewer.

Who Is Billy from Lewiston, Maine, Vanishing in China?

Who am I? When you reach an obscene age
of 87 the reward is wisdom and a big memory
(with lots of holes). Not so bad. I still dance.

And each word I scratch with my ink pen
quivers or flows like my surprise first verse
at dawn of a dark snow Bowdoin night

when a sun bird chirps at the window. I ape
Christopher Isherwood in Berlin Cabaret 30s.
He confirms his act on a postcard he sends

back from Hollywood. Our lifespan is
a sailing wind heading for a black harbor grave
or the dream Ithaca never to be reached.

And guess what. Next week we float
off to Shanghai, *city on the sea*, where
four decades ago, I am sole inhabitant

in the Peace Hotel. Chou Enlai is only
blocks away. He gives my early madness a push.
But even this Malraux-like figure tinkers

worriedly with poems he shares with Nixon
in his Shanghai hideout. Once a Paris 11th
arrondissement radical student, amid the now

bloody Revolution slaughter he keeps dignity
and dangerously tries to lessen the worst.
I turned the Helmsman's 37 poems to English

and wire Chou. Chou wires me: *Go to Ontario
to pick up visa.* Suddenly I am shuffling though
Great Proletarian Cultural Revolution China.

Each morning the Pearl River in Hong fills
with corpses floating down from the People's
Democracy. I see her model ballet *Red Detachement*

of Women at Beijing Opera. My stern comrade
'Little Ripple' comments in King's English:
This joint is really jumpin'. Morning, I behold

the supremely religious Middle Kingdom
of people clad alike in convict gray and blue,
fighting armies, painting heaven with their

blood. By midnight I sneak off from my hosts
get on a trolley, fly like fire in a bamboo forest
all alone in empty China. Strange being

here lost on these ancient alleys of jade
where three emperors came from their village
to find apples of silk in the inner gardens

of sleeping hutong mansions. I hear oil lamps
and panthers and overhead silent night geese.
I knock quietly at a thin dark patio door,

walk in and disappear where each illusion
is snow. In old China my endless first dream
is Tang poet Wang Wei on Deep South

Mountain. He sings the woodcutter he meets
laughing and lost to time. Wang's plain words
are dancing on the earth. So Billy thinks.

Time on the World Tree

Time is, was, and will be whether I am
or not. Our time began with the big boom.
What time before the bang? Only a ham
astrologer sleeping in heaven's room
might say, or ask Franz Kafka, specialist
of the impossible: 'INFINITY
before the pit of Babel, a no-time mist
before clocks start to tick.' My own world tree
of time I borrow while I stay on earth.
I sprinkle water on it, jog to give
my body powers. But after my last breath
(when all insomnia flees) I'll sigh and write
a volume on the beauty of the night.
Though I won't wake, please read and we shall live.

Kabbalah Has a Tree with Surprising Leaves

I gave to Hope a watch of mine, but he
An anchor gave to me.

– George Herbert

Kabbalah has a tree from whose branch hang
Hebrew letters of black fire spelling H O P E,
pretty like the Tree of Life on the ceiling
of the Santo Domingo church in Oaxaca
where volcano climbers cool out with salt
and lemon margaritas. Zapata came through
but back in Catalonia Gershom Sholem worked
on the Sefer HaBahir, the Book of Brightness,
in that illuminated triangle of Gnostic Cathars,
Spanish mystics, and Cabbalists. Word, words

the entrails of a bull. I floated years amid
the unseeable, those late neoplatonists.
They offer me true color, invisible color,
and belief is not the point. The mind
has caverns intuited only in oblivion.
Will we ever wake to Plato's blind sun?
Let winds blow all doors and windows.
Kabbalah has a tree from whose branch hang
Hebrew letters of black fire spelling H O P E.

The World Stuff for the Pre-Socratics

I read and reread the old philosophers
Largely though memory. Obscure Parmenides
Bestows eternal stillness while loud-mouth Heraclitus
(Whom Borges calls *El Greco*, 'the Greek')
Catches rivers dancing. I love dance in marble Greece
Or Seville's Fair smelling of candles to the gorgeous
Inquisition-robed Virgin and all-night flamenco.
Plato the soulman permits music of ascension.
While Atomists coach me in physics (in Latin *natura*),
Towering among the earth's philosophers is the
Ancient Lighthouse of Alexandria who scans the sea.
If I could ask her rubble to waken and scan
The sea in me, I might be an atlas of butterflies
Eager and Kafka-tiny, and with my buggy eyes,
Read and reread the old philosophers.

Baruch Spinoza Embraces Space

Baruch Spinoza always has it right.
There's no divinity above the clouds,
or devil in mid earth below our sight.
Those Bible miracles he drapes in shrouds.
Nature and God are one reality.
He sees all things of our world as divine
from air and stars to generosity
and love. Riches he gives away. He's fine
with poverty and friends, a pipe, a beer
and grinding lenses, although glass dust brings
him early death. The pallid Jew in small
Latin script polishes the wonder, cheer
and mathematics of the mind. Thought wings
him through the night. He loves the tiny all.

Inner Landscape

One year I crawled back through my eyes
To a wider plain. Sweet and stormy!
I wept inside and walked on painful dew.
I swallowed icicles of moonlight. Sharp
Exquisite colors jangled through me—
Citrus dipped in water; flowers white,
Intricate as snowflakes, big as heavy tusks.

One year I sank down to a wider plain,
And always gazing at my frantic feet,
I ran half deaf as if I were
Two giant gargoyles staring face to face.
Those nights were rocked with tugging chains,
Sabers slashed the sky above my sleep,
I could not stand, and tried to crawl

Outside. But change was slow. The mind
Like eyes and muscles holds it scars.
The inner beach is full of flies that stick,
And daybreak surf slides deep in memory.
At night the mutilated blackness burns,
The jagged fountain shines, for change is slow;
For dawn-blue foam's a scare that never fades.

The Lady in the Blue Black Hat

The lady in the blue black hat
displays a marriage of each hue
in Mark Rothko's last paintings that

Howard commissioned to imbue
his Rothko Chapel with a peace
unknown on earth. And when he died

I sat holding a white rose. Please
don't leave. A plain pine box. Inside
my brother drew new plans to make

amazing beauty. Rothko too
chose suicide to still the ache
of shrieking demons. The lady

in the Paris outfit is my wife.
After a gale an ordinary
breeze whispers no or yes to life.

Notes on the Poems

All drawings are by the poet.

Dad and I Go to Mexico
'I Went and Never Leave': '*Que por Mayo era por Mayo, / cuando canta la calandria /y responde el ruiseñ*' ('The lark sings out, the nightingale responds').

Mexico in My Heart
'With Pancho Villa on the Road, 1943': Porfirio Díaz was president/dictator of Mexico (1876–1911). Liberal aristocrat Francisco Madero initiated the Mexican Revolution that overthrew Díaz, aided by Pancho Villa, famous commander of the División del Norte.

Lives of the Poets
'Limping Quevedo Walled in by Time': Saint John of the Cross (1543–1592), mystical poet and Carmelite monk, author of 'Dark Night of the Soul', whose key poems retell The Song of Songs.

'Evening Talk with Borges in Buenos Aires, 1975': '*La bolsa o la vida*, he says, *La vida*.' ('Your wallet or your life', he says. 'My life.')

'From London Horror to a Select New England Campus': the line '*The gendarme came to tell me you had hanged yourself on the door of a rented room*' is from 'Turn Your Eyes Away' in Ruth Stone's *Second-Hand Coat*.

African Bestiary
Each epigraph provides the Swahili word for the animal of the poem.

'The White Unicorn': the Chinese word for 'Unicorn' is *Qilin*.

Poems from Babel
'Maurice Sendak in the Woods': 'a hoax to fool visiting drunken Red Cross officials into thinking the death camp humane': After the Danish and Swiss Red Cross leave, the performing singers and musicians are sent to Auschwitz for execution.

Moonbook and Sunbook
'Gospel of Clouds': The peat bog soldiers were prisoners of war in the Börgerniir Nazi concentration camp in Lower Saxony. The song was composed in German by inmates and sung by thousands of inmates as they marched with their digging spades instead of rifles. It became a resistance song in many languages during World War II. In his resonant voice, Paul Robeson famously sang it both in German and English:

Wir sind die Moorsoldaten
und ziehen mit dem Spaten ins Moor.
Wir sind die Moorsoldaten
und ziehen mit dem Spaten ins Moor.

We are the peat bog soldiers,
Marching with our spades to the moor.
We are the peat bog soldiers,
Marching with our spades to the moor.

'Poètes dans la lune / Poets in the Moon': this poem was originally written in French, the English transition came later.

'Dylan Looks Great, 1953': Saint Vincent's, the Greenwich Village hospital in New York where Dylan Thomas died on 9 November 1953.

'Time On The World Tree' & Other New Poems
'Antonio Machado on a Bench Facing the Sea in Collioure, 1939': When John of the Cross died in 1591 in a monastery in Ùbeda, Spain, his torso and head were sent north to Segovia to be buried in a small chapel cemetery directly below Antonio Machado's window.

Acknowledgements

I wish to thank my family, each in the arts, for being there always: Aliki, Robert, Elli, and Tony. 'Four eyes see better than two', one says in Spanish, and so for their vision and encouragement and also their poems as example and source, I say hello to Vicente Aleixandre, Ruth Stone, Yusef Komunyakaa, Phil Levine, Mark Strand, Stanley Moss, Gerald Stern, Robert Stewart and, for her six eyes, my wife Sarah Handler.

Poems previously published in *ABC of Translation* are reproduced here with the permission of Black Widow Press.

Poems previously published in *Moonbook and Sunbook* are reproduced here with the permission of Tupelo Press.

Poems previously published in *Stickball on 88th Street* are reproduced here with the permission of Red Hen Press.

Poems previously published in *Life Watch* are reprinted with the permission of The Permissions Company, Inc., on behalf of BOA Editions Ltd., www.boaeditions.org

The sequence *Dad and I Go to Mexico* was first published as 'The House of Light' in *New Letters* Vol. 75 no. 4 (Summer, 2009).

Poems previously published in *The Secret Reader*, and the sequence 'Overheard' (from *Algebra of Night: New & Selected Poems, 1884–1998*), reproduced here with the permission of Sheep Meadow Press.

'Poètes dans la lune / Poets in the Moon': first published in *Café de l'Aube à Paris/Dawn Café in Paris* (Sheep Meadow Press, 2011).

Index of Titles

Index of First Lines